The Ghost of the Wooden Squid

D0899700

RANDOM ACTS OF POETRY

BY RYAN BUYNAK

Published by Paradisiac Publishing.
http://www.paradisiacpublishing.com

Coyote Blood, Inc.

Contact:
www.ryanbuynak.com
www.coyoteblood.blogspot.com

Cover Art by Angie Pickman
www.ruralpearl.com

ISBN: 978-0-9853168-0-8

"the Trimurti,
and the goddamn
Devil,
got lost last time...
they ate poetry
and spoke of unobtainable love."

-Puppy Jones, NYC, 2010

FOR

THE ONE

You have to create it or destroy it to live it or love it.

Fuck You

fuck Brooklyn!
and fuck you
for wasting my time
with eyes that shine
like nickels
named after nightmares.

fuck the morning time,
it goes by so slyly
and then the afternoon
lets me down
every single fucking time.

fuck that hat
you used to wear.
I wonder if you still do.
fuck that book
you said was your favorite:
A Confederacy of Dunces.

fuck time and age,
fuck decay, too.
fuck those fuckers
who are weaker than you.

I wonder what time it is on the sun.
remember last night?
devils and angels pounding
on my gates, terribly so.
fuck them assholes
who disturb our parents
after they are dead.

I won't ruin the future.
do you remember last night?

1

magical, indeed, despite
the desert of Manhattan on the horizon
and the noise
and you eating paste
like a goddamned kindergartner.

You Are Welcome

the noose drips off my nose.
trimmed as misery.
my haircut is not a haircut.
and my face won't speak.
hug your bones.

captain oh captain
I have no one to weekend.
I want to shoot off my big ol' mouth.
but I have no one to talk to.

trimmed in cranberry pants.
crackling wood gone white.
garage rock doldrums.
miserable beatnik dreams and sloth severance.
I'm well and writing.

clean the blood off my face.

Love is a Gateway Drug

I love you beautiful.
I love you strange.

The most beautiful woman in the world
is in my southern bed
with her cheeks and her sense of humor.

I am not there.
I am with peacocks and tomahawks.

With a head full of preface lives,
hung heavy with crown, sure as shit.

A vision of addiction
as a scarily arresting serpent world.

The Calculating Genius of Outrage and Sorrow

Life doesn't get easier,
even when it gets easier.

If your legs had lungs,
how far would you run?

Art Money!

Creature, Creature!
tempestuous, to say the least.
I have hard hate for the summer:
clamorous mischief of the soul
and profuse sweating do not mix.

the top dresser drawer,
theoretically for socks,
also holds the eccentricities
of a language in letters
and many inside jokes.

we are inside a lightning storm.

I still hate olives.

in this atmospheric mix
of bold adventure
and grand romance...

even though,
in this world
you cannot win,
we learn north
and try
being
stronger than last year.

Winter

work,
bad days,
bad dreams,
broken tv,
radio,
The Antlers,
foolishness,
missing her,
illness,
work,
evil people,
staring at bears,
winter...

that is the short of it.

how's it going with you?

snowy television,
feeling too old,
immature,
The Dodos,
work,
missing me, too,
demons,
the dermatologist,

water a Saturday
(morning like river,
one-hundred December)...

the days spend us both.

money, alone.
randomness, surrender.

that room, ago.
too much to drink.
thunder, doubt.
still Young, dumb.
royal smiles,
fake hatred, cold,
never knowing.

Lava

lines, lines, lines...
some are crossed,
some are cut up with credit cards
and white.

this one is about riding bikes.
the next one is about the next life.
knives are instruments of philosophy.

(and love is no fluke lava)

Poem

woke up around noon
turned on an old Scott Walker LP
and then wrote some poetry
on an old receipt, this:

I can't live this way forever.
And I do not want to.

House Mountain

ma'am,
mosey on over here
with that hidden hatchet
and chop my heart in half.

love is for losers,
and,
yet,
despite wishes on the windshield
and the goddamn rocking chair,
I chose you.

we all have our moments.

measure my tongue
for lies.
measure my will
for endurance.
weigh the halves of my heart
for truth.

Holy Neck Bones
        (It's For Foyil)

...at the end of the night
we've all seen better days.

loser, tail end of winter,
I write for fear of silence.

rumor has it
I was borne
on the pavement
of Rue Sherbrooke
in Montreal.

part live bird, part dead minnow.

now is...now.
now is later, too.
the past was a now.
once was a now.

technically day dreaming
at night
at the pub alone,
writing,
5ish, selfish,
the sun disappearing behind my side ribs,
and I can feel
the couple left next to me
judging me.

I keep looking
at my cellular telephone
waiting for a call
or a textmessage
(my life has repaired to waiting),
despite the fact
that I hate telephones
more than I hate
olives and Nazis.

I cannot shake this.

waiting.
Kings of Leon
come on the juke,
making me a little happier.
Corey keeps the whiskey coming.
I embrace the role
of the lonely loser,
and proceed to get shitty.

if there is no such thing
as time,
we are already there.

the end of streets and shooting stars
are the same thing,
in essence.

prepare myself for another life.

in the belly of a hut march.

in the belly of an airplane.
over rivers.
over the past.

late last night.

wild dogs was I.

Spanish Steve introduced
me to tonight's yak,
and I feel like a kitchen
in the 90s.

I am instantly unforgiven.
no meals.
I am a loud boombox.
the first and the fifteenth
of the month.
niggas get tired.
my whole perspective is fucked.
sometimes you are holy,
better,
I think.

Knees

Rain knees.
Sunday afternoon knees.
Skateboard knees.
Potato food.
Bank robberies.
Go on living.

Document 4

Some stories start like this...

Petrichor.
Rebellion: Dandelion.
ravenouscontinuesnext.

The Prologue of it all:
this is a story of loss...
aren't they all?
After all,
poets only write about love, life and death,
all of which are documents lost.

Anonymous and found,
first-floor pages, burned in shirt-waist fires,
years later,
filing cabinets,
forgotten then found.

I would say the closest thing to it
is when you think you are nothing but
the bitter spin of the gone wilderness,
and time; so be it;
if the living room comes to me, fair enough,
the chance to cut as a chance to cure!

Sticky collar bones above broken heart dense longitude,
loose love behind the Pub,
Joe's two or three packs a night.
I am Abe Lincoln, I am Shiva: Sick and...
very nice and as interesting as an airport
but I come from the land of the sun! (!)

Nothing about today made sense to me.

Last night I lost her tonight.
I woke up twice for good,
last night and forever.

Life is good, I guess.
Black people invented rock-n-roll.
Boats exist.
Giraffes, too.
For now.
We are young.
For now.

The Kaleidoscope Kid and I.

We buzzed Jeffa's apartment.
He calls down and asks who it is.
"It's Richard and Jacob," Jacob says.
"I know Richard but who is Jacob?" Jeffa calls back
down.
"The Kaleidoscope Kid." Jacob says sheepishly.
Then the buzzer sounds and we are in the building,
and walking up six flights of stairs
so by the time we reach the drug dealer's floor
we are panting and sweating like narcs.

I knock once, nothing.
Jacob knocks twice and Jeffa opens the door.
Jeffa is a pale dude with pale hair.
He is from Florida, too.
He is shirtless.
He is a Hugo Boss model
and a dancer
and a pusher.

"Well if it isn't the Kaleidoscope Kid and the fucking
poet!"

Jeffa sparks a bowl and tells some bullshit story,
most drug dealers are lonely hyperbolists.

Life is a bunch of fuckin' colors.

This is not the end.

Saoirse and I take the train downtown
and we are forced to take the local;
the express is not running
because of some stupid suicide casualty at 125th street.

The hard earth is full of good humans,
but only a select few are great...
and then they are gone,
turning into ex-girlfriends
or landlords or nincompoops
or microphones of memories.
All killers of some kind, or victims of another kind.
the dynamic has changed
and the good brassers
have gone their merry way
in motorcade fashion.

I take my time to cross Bleecker Street.

We
catch up with them, The Glorious Veins, at nighttime
lunch in another lifetime,
eat the white paper ravens and the pineapples made of
yarn
with forks and hammers and exclamation points as
utensils,
and sentences without spaces fill the stratosphere.

I will surely freeze to death in the middle
of an interrupted story.

During the show,
some girl said to me: "I like your style."
"I love you with all my heart," I said.

Parts Four and Five and Six and Seven are about Love.
And drugs.
And inside jokes.
H's and K's.

And Document 4 ends like this.

True Face

A man.
An ox.
A lion.
And/or an eagle.

Black is the color of my love.
Black is the color of only a human's blood.

I don't want to die anymore time(s).
But if I do.
I'd still ask to see her and a few.
Things, One more time.

Rain is rain.
In autumn.
In summer.
Coming through screen door or grave.

I am the being
for whom
being is still a question.
I am pleased with my existence.

I am a man just like Ed Gein.
I am a man just like Bapu.

Only Riot Weather

pejorative.
deftly.
surreptitious.
hopelessness.

Miri the Kid

Curious about me
and I about her.

Zero apathy
on both our parts.

Her heart seems as malleable
as funny as clay as life writ large.

The sight of her singing
makes afternoon cats
run towards
her in the living room.

She is a thimble.
Her heart is larger than anyone's.

She is the colored kid,
as her grandmother says,
on the picnic bench,
bright as the day today and tomorrow.

Quite a life she will lead,
opportunistic at best
at its worst at its loudest,
definitely not quiet,
not not silly,
not not singing,
a good ruin
still good, still in use,
saving the future.

I envy her way to the sea,
on the back of a window
on the back of a Stegosauras

on this side of the moon.

She has the kindest heart, beating, signified.

Running Stop Signs

push the heart.
go. go. go.
free the translation of the heart.
for there are.
so many words to say, Spanish and English.

freely, freely,
un corizon.

catch your breath.
wait, for art says it all.
there are so many things I want to remember.
it is raining in Kansas City
and I wish I wrote certain things.

something's happening
and I'll try to put your pages back.
what'd it do?
Page 32.
I've been advertising sleep at night,
because it's been skipped over with life, lately.

seriously consider.
the country of nigh naught.
as it seems.
from windows of a train.
on my way to something happening.
something grand.

Something truly great.

Curtain Thompson
(An Inside Joke, Go Fuck Yourself)

My tooth feels loose.
I haven't been to LA
since last summer,
and before that,
the summer of fear of 2005,
the year I deserved LA,
and now my tooth
feels loose, here, a lifetime later, in NYC.

I gotta pee so badly, too.
The tv is muted.
I pee sitting down.
I woke up sweating last night.
I also dreamed of babies,
and Lake Underhill Road shrinking and blowing up.
It's no surprise
now that I am an addict,
and everyone is an enemy.
This is the Curtain Thompson.

Repent and get over it,
I say over and over again
to my invisible son in said dream.
Today, I take off my brown shoe,
and try to explain to her and her,
the timing never seeming right.
I am a rope, she is my neck.
We both know what to expect
from this stalematesilenttongue.
I don't know where to begin.

I am a hammer.
She is a window.
My tooth feels loose

here in NYC.
Five years seems like forever.
With bargains so sharp
and manholes open
and dreams impatient,
learning not on me to be me;
I never let anyone save me.
I am an exclamation point balloon.
She is a fork.
Or a ghost for now, deservingly, so.

Beginning with Breathing

Understanding the rain...

Mississippi times.
Mississippi fear.

I was never kind.
I've heard better sermons.
I drank a lot of whiskey on those nights.
And red wine in the mornings.

I said on that so-long-ago
Sunday that:
"She's got to taste me
to trust me."

And that was
last night's last night
but it was not the last night
nor will it ever be

Keep me sane, baby,
down my soul.
We fight so high
on barbed wire tight ropes.

She eclipses me
on this sleepy street vacation
somewhere where they
can't crash.

Slip, make love!
Owe the sun!
Cut my sin!
Since December!

Mississippi times.
Mississippi fear.

...But it's not raining.

Your Apartment

Your apartment is in Brooklyn.
We got super high
in your apartment.
Fourth floor, walk-up.
I've written you thirteen-hundred poems since then,
but you will never read any.
This is one of them.
I remember your radiator in the dark,
looking like a monster.
Ask your bookshelf its problems, right?
You were gorgeous in your apartment,
standing still,
in old jeans and yellow wife-beater.
You put on a Joanna Newsome mp3.
I am not falling for this.
We danced our way into the kitchen.
We made love at the table.
We made love in the shower.
I used your apricot scrub.
I will thank you one day for this day,
but not now;
we dry off and burn basil in the kitchen
and pretend dinner was the goal.
I ask the linoleum floor to change, it does not.
You were cunning, oh so cunning,
in your apartment.
You are still shackled to your craziness.
You say five years is not that bad.
I fell for every syllable of that shit.
We guess at the future.
Again.
I will have a story to tell,
but you will tell it differently,
one day.
Now we finally see, proof in pictures in boxes.

We are fictions forced into arranged marriages.
You say six years is nothing.
I cannot believe it has been that long.

Poem

I.

Turn.
Envy.

Where it's deep.
Knowledge by time.

And.

What all of my poor lovers guess.
The right thing is farewell.

Always.

In stars and stairs and men.

Like me.
fickle.

Interlude(s), 2009

January, it is always January.
Applied for a thousand jobs.
Got two.
Saw Cady Wire play at the Basement.
Bought a chair from my buddy Mike.
Got a tattoo of a window.
Sent poetry to ten magazines in America.
And one in Ireland and one in Canada.
Almost got into a fight with Tao Lin on Carmine Street.
Obama's inauguration, Gabe's birthday.
Spent the night with a girl named Somewhere.
Honestly, that was her real name.
I made her show me her license.
Watched ten hours of television.
Saw Kings of Leon at Madison Square Garden.

February and March, bought a bong, had jury duty.
Bought a book on folk guitars, bought a book on rooftop
gardening.
Don't have a rooftop.
Spoke to Laurie on the phone for the first time in years.
Did my w2s, went to Florida.
Spoke to Felipe on the phone for the first time in years.
Made collage art.
Smoked weed with the willful Philly Matt.
Went to a reading at a place called Perch in Brooklyn.
Ran into Robyn, gave her a kiss on the mouth, but
didn't really mean to.
Think about moving, think about running away.
Feature-reading at Cornelia Street Café, a half-assed
Hunter S. Thompson Tribute Night.
I got drunk on regrets.
Dan Morton's birthday, punk rock, borrowed movies
from Avery.

April and May, routine was the thing.
Not washing my hair, don't know why.
Wrote Dan Morton a letter, apologizing for missing his birthday.
Called a girl named Rachel.
Saw Tucksy play at the Basement.
Went to an open mic at the St. Marks Theater.
Paid my debts, bought a camera.
Poem in my pocket day.
Performed in a Kerouac play.
Buddha's birthday.
South Delaware Street, Lindenhurst, NY.
My little sister's college graduation.
Saw Manchester Orchestra in New Jersey.
Ran into Robyn, again.
My little sister's birthday.
Erol's birthday.
Everyday is someone's birthday, literally.
Working a double at the restaurant and fucked for forgetting birthdays.

June, three cheers for hellfire.
Made a Facebook account.
Saw a Snow Leopard at the Central Park Zoo.
A girl called Somewhere's birthday.
California!!!
Flew into San Francisco.
Went to City Lights Bookstore.
Drove over the Golden Gate Bridge thirteen times.
Remember L.A.
Silverlake and Book Soup.
Get high and drive in the hills.
Almost hit a coyote, how ironic.
The flight back to NYC was the scariest flight of my life.
Turbulence to say the least.

July, may times burn bright like before.

33

Met a girl named Mandy at the Heartland Brewery in Union Square.
She is stupid and easy.
Mandy finds me on Facebook.
Got a call from Dan.
Got a call from Gabe.
Saw Trevor Hall play at The Bell House.
Call Matt English, he doesn't answer.
Matt English calls me back.
Cocaine and Ketamine and kicking over a Vespa.
Tomorrow.
Symphony in Central Park, 8pm.
Run into the girl called Somewhere.
Poetry gig in Long Island, her again.
Find leftover cocaine in nightstand.

August, I will be one of the goofy ones in the back of the business.
Overheard terrible things about minors at a restaurant.
Found out about The Drums, from Florida.
Opened for The Glorious Veins on a rooftop somewhere in Brooklyn.
Don't know how I got home.
Don't know how I worked a double at the restaurant the next day.
Poetry gig in Springfield, Massachusetts.
Went skateboarding for the first time in years.
Bought tickets to see Edward Sharpe and the Magnetic Zeros.
Wrote like crazy, due to that long leftover cocaine.
Beat it, to start it, the heart.
Read Shakespeare's *Measure for Measure*.
Ran into Sam and she said again I am too self-aware.

September and October, listless and self-congratulatory, for now.
While pissing wrote on the bathroom wall of the Music

Hall of Williamsburg.

"Coyote Blood Will Kill You!"

Got a negative evaluation at the restaurant.

I want to be Brian Austin Greene

Finished "Gabe's Birthday" story.

Joined a gym, just to play basketball.

Tell Somewhere that I can't do dinner.

Don't know why.

Little Danny from Orlando comes to visit.

Wrote a long poem about the plastic Beatles dolls my
mom used to have in a hutch.

Florida, new Pearl Jam album.

Working a double at the restaurant.

Chris Corso's birthday.

My birthday!

The devil in my throat.

Do not call her.

Do not call her.

Hang out with PQ and Gabe, like old times.

First check from the book, in the mail.

Cash it, and spend it on drugs.

Got a second job at a café on 68th and Central Park
West.

Saw Gasoline Heart play somewhere in Brooklyn.

Stole olive oil and bread and milk from the new job.

Sam's birthday.

Met a girl at Grey Dog Café near Union Square.

I forget her name and her face.

Read Frank O'Connor and got drunk.

Read Lorca and got high.

Got fired from new job for stealing.

November, the road is gonna end.

Basketball season is underway, indeed.

Do not call her.

Do not call her.

Dusk with a limp.

728 is the new numeric signal for cocaine.
Day of the Dead.
Poetry gig in Montreal, took a train.
Rue Sherbrooke, Rue LaMontagne.
One of two English speaking poets.
Watched too much tv.
Went to Robyn's play in Union Square.
Called Barbara, she didn't pick up.
Saw Metallica at Madison Square Garden.
Anniversary of some kind, Cookie Esteban's special
voice message.
Saw Devendra Banhart play at TownHall.
Big sister visits for a week.
Nothing but brunches and bbqs.
Thanksgiving Day, thanks.

Love is a week in December.
Snow.
Do not call her.
Do not call her.
Bob Hart's show in Union Square.
Christmas Shopping done early.
Draw an upside down alligator, and a sideways serious
giraffe.
Glow in the dark.
Bought a Bob Dylan t-shirt for the girl called
Somewhere.
Don't know why.
Mail it to her.
Employee Christmas party.
Working a double at the restaurant.
Read Bukowski.
Pissed my pants.
Kissed the concrete.
Drank too much, watched too much tv.
Snow.

Beautiful Cynical Rot

In the debut dark of the night,
I hear a whispered voice
calling my name.

It calls this the beginning,
as I spin too finite
with a brand new name.

Dead be me
and birth be fire,
my finger nails leave.

Sternum is open,
seatbelts are broken,
I am a consumer good of the gone earth.

My bones rattle
and I taste it
in my ribs, the greatest.

Also, I watch
as my eyes are eaten
by seahorses.

I am done for,
stupid and salty,
a casualty of the blood and denim.

Cast a shadow
of bitten hips
in sawgrass ditches in which I lay.

Not for long,
browning and scalped,
a tomahawk jones.

Left and leaving,
the future came too soon, Turkey Vultures, too.
Verve was enough.

They Called It a Scene, I Call It a Disaster

white ghettos were unannounced and overlooked
in those days, they still are.

still working at the restaurant.
always and never.

never forever.

once an artist, always poor.

I need to take a type O shit
in the gut veins
with eye teeth
and egg holes.

I close both, all (none)
forces from the world,
but not the toe nose.

how can I say this truth
is better than art?

because it *is*.

a bastard waiter.
a blind hobo.
they both sleep.
and shit.
writers are thieves,
jack rabbits, indeed,
slim as no anorexic should be
within heroin memories
and bubblegum doldrums
from youth in white ghettos
of trailer park Central Florida,

39

Taft hood, under Regan,
absentee Dads,
now dead
and written about here
with soundtrack and hyperbole.

Poem, Mix CD 888

16. *St. Augustine* by Band of Horses
17. *Disconnected* by Face to Face
18. *Kansas in the Spring* by Truckstop Honeymoon
19. *A Change Gonna Come* by Sam Cooke
20. *Charlie Darwin* by The Low Anthem

The Incident

what,
with waking up with
scratches on my face
and a bump on my head,
with vomit and women's
underwear in my bed,
with dried blood in my mustache,
with a big bag of cocaine
in the pocket of last night's jeans,
from where it came I have no idea,
with the absence of money from my wallet,
with a broken cellphone,
the pieces of which are all
over my kitchen floor,
and my front door is wide open...

I do not want to remember last night.

The Old Age of Youth

Guitar my kitchen.
Goddamn time.
With hands of the clock so bloody.

From tulips and stopping-by-after-work.
Come on, Laser Lips.
Let me up, feel seventeen.
Again.

Beers in my feet.
Now is always now.
It was never then.
At ease.
With what I don't want to do.

Why is it that
my back hurts every Thursday?
Sad folk songs.
In my aforementioned kitchen.
heard down the hall.
Outside.

The park is dark.
The subway is rumbling.
We call it the *Rumbler*.
She calls it that.
A sixpack and laughter.
Folks fall far.
My bestfriends are having a baby.

You will find
that these years are mean
in life,
even to a new born
or a twenty-nine year old poet

Kick The Bucket

last night the devil stole the moon
while Vernon and I and Matt English
were snorting cocaine in the kitchen
and the police were all over Harlem
looking for a serial rapist.

this is the future, they say,
and someone kicks the bucket
every thirteen seconds.

one,
two,
three,
four,
five,
six,
seven,
eight,
nine,
ten,
eleven,
twelve,
thirteen.

my hands sweat
and my mouth runs on diesel fuel
until four in the morning
and paranoia is king, here.

now I sit at home and pretend
that I won't ever kick the bucket
while Vernon and Matt English
are doing the exact same thing, somewhere.

we are martyrs of some kind, doubtless,

but I can't figure out the godspeed angle.
or why.

Gorgeous Girls

gorgeous girls are like that,
they think they can just grab your beard
over breakfast on a Monday morning
when you haven't seen each other in a year
since she left on tour with a play to Minnesota and
Wisconsin.

gorgeous girls are like that,
they think they can just stare at you in taxi cabs
with their big beautiful brownish blue eyes
in the awkwardly amazing afternoon light
driving uptown along the Hudson River.
gorgeous girls are like that,
they think they can just grab your hand
while crossing the street at 92nd and Broadway
in the dusk red dim glow
of the best day of your life.

because...oh, she slays me...oh, her again.

We Are All Liars

I write lies.
I tell poetry.

I produce philosophy
sometimes
when I am not too drunk.

I tell tall tales
at work or at a party
to
people more stupid than myself.

There are lines
in my face
new ones in the mirrorwworld
some I wish I could change.

I milk the sun
with sleep and meat
and each reddest red is mine.

I hate your taste in music,
yes you,
all of you.

I love your lips
as you introduce yourself as Ms. Somewhere,
and smitten am I, forever.

Always as always,
like a loop in time,
this life is the same
as the last life as mine.

When I was young,

I dreamed of being a liar
and a drunk and a poet.

I live in New York City
and I am deliciously drunk
right this very moment.

Living the iniquitous dream,
smooth and serious,
truly, adore (that is a good word) this moment in time.

the gunshots
don't bother me,
nor does the brain hurricane or the static.

yesterday I fell in love with a stranger
and the day before that I did the same thing
with a completely different stranger on the subway.

I tell poetry.
I write lies.

I kick and ugly cry when I am excited
in the air wherever I am in the world.

jump from reggae to folk music
with quick hand
and three-time heart.

come home drunk
and lost as usual,
forget to eat, but smoke, get online.

There are lines
in my face
new ones in the mirrorwworld
some I wish I could change.

48

de ja vu.
yesterday I fell in love.
I write lies.

Everybody Same Time Leave

I am from a place
called Fireplug, Florida,
where dirty bones live in the
same zipcodes as their parents,
who are divorced born-again Christians,
and they
slap the love that you left,
and they
start each scene
with the slamming of a door,
and excuses and strong drink.

I am not scared anymore
and that, my friends, is
the scariest thing of all.

I am taller than a buzzard,
bigger than a breadbox;
some One is testing me.

I deserve to die.
Everyone does.

Midnight Lions

This river,
this river
is as old as I,
it makes me concerning of Brooklyn
and her smell on the 100th of January.

Do rivers cast shadows?
Do rivers hold on to pessimism?

Oh! this is what the man in me thinks about
when trying to fall into sleep.
Or death.

Morning lambs or midnight lions?

Last week's rivers,
over which we kissed?

Every beat of my alkaloid heart
as every blink of her eyes.

Oh! sleep is overrated.

Ark

the animals,
all of the themes,
wild nor wonderful,
said *Rejoice*.

Clementine

Thiago from Brazil.
Marty from Canada.
and me.

I'm the one tossing a clementine up into the air and
catching it again.

I emailed her an hour ago.
Right before we left for the bar.

Marty keeps calling me a pussy.
Thiago doesn't give a shit about love.

I give the clementine to a hobo.

The hobo asks what it is.
Thiago says it's love.
Marty calls it a tangerine.

Poem

Is it altogether
possible to have
more than one soulmate
in this sweet world?

I forgot to brush my teeth today.

Anything is possible.

Goodnight, Sarah

She manages a restaurant
six days a night.
She is in love with someone
who doesn't love her the same way.
She does dance.
She does drugs.
She says she is fine
but she gets high and
talks about herself in
the third person, Suicide Sarah.
She says she wants to move with her
brother to Missouri and own a farm,
but, then again, she says a lot of things.
She sucked a stranger's dick
on the night of her twenty-sixth birthday.
She says she wants to stop smoking.
She says she wants to
be better at life.
She says her StepMom sends
her self-help books in the mail.
She says her StepMom doesn't understand her.
Sarah sometimes stares at the sun out of spite.
Sarah has taught herself to write in reverse.
She says she doesn't
have a favorite song
or a favorite film.
She talks to herself sometimes.
She says she feels like a sewer or, at best, a drainpipe.
She says I don't understand.
She is wrong in so many ways.

Poem, Mix CD 888

11. *Love is All I Am* by Dawes
12. *Skinny Love by* Bon Iver
13. *Sleepwalker* by Johnny and Santo
14. *Your House* by Jimmy Eat World
15. *Bushwick Blues* by Delta Spirit

Kinesthetic

Macho,
picture man,
meet the longleaf father.

Take his only-parent photo.

Ask him what means the most to him.
Shake his hand.
Look him in the eye.

Watch how the miserable mother dances.
With her head and her arms.
Walk with her side ribs.
Wake up without.

Pick up the kids.

Hope until you die.

Drive to the store.
Groceries.

Forest Hills, What The Fuck?

Penn Station, track 18, 3:46pm
train to Forrest Hills,
18 degrees in Queens.

I wonder what life is like living in Forest Hills.
Probably the same as everywhere else in America,
or the world for that matter:

work, live, try to find some sort of love,
eat, shit, die, blink, get sick, get better,
have babies, etc, etc, etc.

My friend Gabe lives in Forest Hills.
with his girlfriend Nikki.
She works at a restaurant,
he sells weed.

The Fall

I fell backwards,
down the stairs of the Arclight Theater.
I was drunk, she wasn't.
We were going to see some shitty romantic comedy, her
choice.
I had gotten drunk in the hotel bar beforehand.
Because...well, because I was a bit nervous.
I hadn't seen her in six years, maybe eight.
She then she had to drive us.
She said she wasn't mad,
But I knew she was very mad.
You can always tell a girl is mad
when she says she is not mad over and over.
I tested her by spitting out of the window of the car.
I thought this might push her over the edge.
Except, I had forgotten to roll the window down.
Saliva splash! Luckily, it was a rental.
We were at a stoplight on Sunset and Lacienega.
The kids in the car next to us saw me spit on the inside
of the window.
The all got a good laugh.
I lit a joint, rolled the window up and down a bunch of
times with the punch of a button, and, to my surprise,
she stole the cone joint away from my hand.
She puffed on it a few times and then flicked it out the
driver's side window.
I only had five bucks on me,
and I used that to pay for parking.
And I had lost my debit card a few nights
before at a pub somewhere in Silver Lake.
Before three days ago, hadn't had a drink in a long
time.
I hadn't had a dream worth remembering either.
When I fell in the lobby, while dancing up the stairs,
the maroon carpeting

burned my back badly, but I pretended it didn't hurt.
Instinctively, I waited for someone to help me up.
Once I got myself up, she was nowhere in sight,
just a room full of big eyes.
So, I ended up seeing *Sex and the City 2*
by myself.

Why So Dark So Early?

I think my brain is swelling
on a Thursday night,
nine nurses and two criminals in,
selfish at best,
like the kazoo.

She dances to Pearl Jam while putting in a tampon
on a Thursday night,
two valiums and one glass of redwine in,
enamored and windowbeautiful,
like life's exclamation point.

I live in violence-occasionally-happens.
She in splendor.
I am tragedy-occurs.
I of New York City.
She has figured out how to freeze time.

The hammer breaks the window;
brand new to childhood,
we grow backwards with the nights
so permanently loud.

When will I give a fuck about anything?

Criers' Contest

since we're here,

you've said I am heartless
so many times.
maybe I am, 12%.

it has been such a busy
introspective winter
with sad music,
but boo fucking hoo, right?

my brain is bleeding, probably.

We're not too old
to re-fall in love.
We are professional humans
with exquisite tear ducts
and shadowy souls.

Anklers' Meeting

in toilet with three ladybugs.
still alive.
please don't forget.
Me.
wishbone drawbridges, too.

come hunker.
oh, my shoulder.
in thy nook.
be ashes, be cornmeal, be veins.

both in terms of evidence and experience.
the dungeon of the human figure.
in wicker chairs.
in whiskey bottle fatigue.

Brooklyn is so right, Wednesdays ago,
as October's day's night,
moving in the something
like a ball bouncing on the floor.

ten twenty five Monday morning afterward.
two days before.
flight number eighteen forty five.
from NYC to Orlando, back in time.

Keep floatin'.
All the way to Illinois,
to Austin, from Florida.

Keep floatin'.
All the way to someplace,
and All the way back again.

The sun reads over my shoulder

63

through a cabin window of a Boeing
which Won't shut because some kid
in some recent day Stuck gum in the hinges.

The birds fly low in Austin,
where I floated from bar to bar
and in one, I met a punkrock poet
called Tommy, he had a green
Dropkick Murphys t-shirt on and
I think he was homeless, but he was a sweetheart,
and
He never hesistated giving up his cigarettes.

Alone.

U.F.O.

Dejé a mi familia al atardecer.

He pagado un hombre con un camión

cincuenta dólares americanos

me llevan a través de la frontera.

Dormía en un sonajero de serpiente selva

saltó de un tren en Arizona.

ocho personas que viven en un sótano.

Dios mio.

corte de césped o lavar los platos.

Dios mio.

el diablo se esconde detrás de los copos de nieve.

Soy muy frío.

reloj me desaparecen.

Poem, Mix CD 888

1. *Jellybones* by The Unicorns
2. *Buriedfed* by Miles Benjamin Anthony Robinson
3. *Hoboken* by Operation Ivy
4. *St. Joseph's* by The Avett Brothers
5. *Molly* by Sponge

Song of the Busboy

in the eyes of senator strangers,
they are help, just.
they are not blue-collar,
but they are not parking lot attendants.

no one wants to hear their stories anymore,
omelets and cigarettes,
maintenance and tv sets,
who has time for romance?

in these United States
along this Gulf of Mexico,
going to Community College,
illegal as can be.

this is the song of the busboy
playing five nights a week
sometimes six, depending
if someone needs a shift covered.

The Death Bridge

Out of town...
an Island,
a mainland,
and
me,
a limestone peninsula.

My cancerous granddaddy
has his tombstone already picked out.

The ground is brown
and the earth is blue.

No wonder.
No wonder.

My girl's heart
told her head this
time: maybe
(in a year).

Me,
and love,
as it was
made to be,
to be set free
(or set on fire).

Airport Bars

ahhhhhh, airport bars,
love 'em.
my brother loves 'em, too.

the beers are small and expensive.
it's always too early or too late.
it's always breakfast and lunch.

girls like Jessicas
from the Midwest
with muscular necks,
quoting last week's *Saturday Night Live*.
they flirt but they don't.
all the Jessicas are married,
their husbands are named Peters or Rons
or Aarons or Chris or Larry,
and they are all away on business
in places like Portland or Tampa.

I buy a Jessica a bloody mary.
She laughs at my jokes.

The Time-In Devil

This is a Mjöllnir.
Posing as a haircut.
Posing as a window.
Posing as the arms.
Into which you fall and curse.

This is an exclamation point.
Posing as mountains.
Posing as the end.
Posing as the time-in
Devil.

This is a fork.
Posing as an arrow.
Posing as a coward.
Posing as a red river.
Which may or may not run dry.

The telephone gave us hope.
Hammers gave us breakfast.

Between the Parties That Supersede Certain Things

Blue me
and orange me,
middle school me.
Red and brown me,
gold lux me.
Glass my heart.
Midnight me.
Fuse to me,
base.
Ten color me.
Fuck me.

Cum off at the end there.
Right up above my gorgeous hip.
My hands made of glass,
like my heart,
sweating and on fire.
And still burning years later.
Even through half asleep.
Buried and finished.
Hungry and needing a cigarette.
Lost and limp and in love, still.

The soft-worded letter I wrote her
with my thick, crack-knuckled hand
was returned to my sister's place
a decade and a week and a day ago.
She called me four minutes ago,
near four in the morning,
but did not leave a message.
She has to be in Buffalo, right?
Righting some wrongs,
writing some songs.

She cut her hair, I heard.

71

Poem

I am not a believer.

I am littered with the night.
And allowed in the kitchen.
Only sometimes...

Sleep may kill me.
The lightbulbs flicker.

I just finished healing.

Sometimes Owls

to you,
everfelt headless clouds
without self to be you
so scared of death,
wealth is death,
fear is your hourly heart
wayward as it is,
not never-ending like the summer rain,
and holy
unlike the pigeons
with their bravado and pride,
they die too,
watchers know this.

may the equator
serve as evertried
ties till noon
all
that hold onto the center steam
all
that they fly south and dream,
hooks in mouths, always beaches,
view the god-owned morning
causing legs and eggs and arms as wings
still having feathers,
today is the day, always,
laws benign with beaks.

accidentally electrocuted,
those
that cannot shock the wake up
institution within dharma doldrums,
capsized the future
like talon-rote in booklet caves
please,

trust the history to you,
the one without lips
but with the big eyes
and the beautiful back like an owlet.

keep you in a box,
collected at borders
knowing not so long as much
fancy the fibs or not,
all that whose
red-breasted benevolence,
hollow bones,
who
wage warfare-hope to be,
yet whose little copper charges
can't seek
and
can't talk to the dead.

Envy the wayward pigeon,
grabbing for grubs and garbage,
swooping and shitting,
without the faintest hint of the fear of death...
all besides that primal last-second instinctual,
the shock, and the evolutionary avoidance of danger-
things.
The pigeon doesn't write about death,
the pigeon doesn't know it's life will end no matter
what.
The wayward pigeon is not afraid of death...
like me.

Sorry

The phone call travels
from her sister's place in Tennessee
to me in New York City,
from cocaine coughs
to bathroom sit-ups
and back to prescription pills
and random, unseasonable rain
where once boats were with her,
as was I.

I kill these six-year phone calls,
blaming airplanes
and satellites,
because I am vain
and once I spilled ketchup
faked for desks
and old fuck buddies,
made of mistakes
and regrets, maybe

I crack my knuckles
as I lean on cardboard questions,
looked upon by distant
friends who pat each other on
the goddamn back, pretending
patience and loving it all,
drunk dialing and wanting
back time, buck, rex, fuck, abortions.

Later, years, sitting at scotch bar
with beer and convoluted contemplation,
and it sounds like
we would have had grand years
if it weren't for each other.

I wonder why
she never leaves a voice message
and whether it
would have been worth it all.
I loved the shit outta her.
Once.
I miss her now more than that.

He

Whatever he had with her,
he didn't have this with her
and he didn't know what love is
and he didn't know you.

He was a liar,
but he was benevolent
in prison or hell.

He was the king of double standards.

He tried to be good,
but he just wasn't good at it.

He left behind postage stamps and a stolen notebook,
using only twenty four pages:
nothing but shitty words
and horrible hand-drawn pictures,
no improving plans of humanization,
just absent wishing and complaining
and drawings of hammers and ghosts.

Hope his daughter doesn't see this shit
in the future.
After
he has coughed himself to death.

Immemorial

Erol and I gave up and gave in and bought tickets
online three days before the actual show; I put them on
my credit card (Erol still owes me the money).

Forty hours later, a wet Wednesday, Erol and I took the
4 train to Union Square, and then we took the L to
Brooklyn. The L took a while and to our left was a crazy
hobo screaming about the world ending in 50 years.

I'll be dead in fifty years, I thought to myself.

To our right, two officers of the NYPD were arresting a
brown man for some...thing in his possession. Welcome
to New York City, Erol. The subway train was one of
the new ones with the sideways digital stop watch of
destinations, ticking off the stops, in alarm-clock
fashion... until we got off at Bedford Ave.

I hate Brooklyn.

Erol and I took a right on N. 6th and ducked into a pub
called The Loving Cup. We drank PBRs, which came
with a shot of whiskey. It was bum juice but it was
included. I limited myself to two shots of the shitty
whiskey and stuck to the PBRs, mostly.
Erol stayed true and downed about five beers and
seven shots of whiskey; I gave him mine.
Then, all of a sudden, there was a tap on my right
shoulder, and, low and behold, I turn around to see the
gorgeous re-constitutionalized face of my ex-girlfriend,
Sally, in my peripheral. She kissed my cheek and I
kissed hers, and it was soft, just how I remember it, in
her Long Island living room, oh so many years ago.
Turns out, she too was going to see Edward Sharpe and
The Magnetic Zeros at the Music Hall of Williamsburg! I

sulked, but hoped she couldn't see me sulking. Her and I took a shot of whiskey – this time it was Knob Creek, not the bum juice – and we exchanged pleasantries and I met some dude she was with, a douchebag with red hair and tight jeans and a stupid hat and a limp handshake. Erol and I left soon after she touched my mustache (in front of her dude).

We got to the show just as the opening act finished their first song. I forget their name, but they were some space-folk act from Florida. Erol and I ordered Red Stripes and cheersed our beers and leaned on the bar. We were startled by our mutual friend, Vernon, who ran up to us like a devil buffalo with hugs and high-fives and screams and stories and laughter and a giant pillow of cocaine. We went to the bathroom and did lines off the back of one of the toilets and then, in single file, went back to the bar and ordered two beers each and tried to stand up straight.

In a manic rotation, and "To set our spirits free!" as Vernon put it, we went back and forth to the bathroom, taking keybumps of good New York via Colombia or Mexico cocaine with our keys, the ones to the front doors of our apartments, respectively.
I told Vernon about seeing Sally and he hugged me and high-fived me and then we ordered more beers, and Vernon wanted to do a shot. We did a shot of Maker's and then each of us went to the bathroom to do another keybump or two.

Edward Sharpe and The Magnetic Zeros came on the stage of the Music Hall of Williamsburg and we cheered and danced. I could not stop dancing. Vernon disappeared first. I lost Erol right about the start of the third song. I went deeper into the crowd and he stayed behind because, as he has come to declare, his legs would not work. The band was great, but the cocaine wore off with all the dancing, and the fact that I saw my ex-girlfriend again, this time dancing with her douchebag, and so I ventured back to the bar to try to find Vernon, for more of his free blow and a shoulder on which to lean, and to get another drink, of course. I ordered another Red Stripe, but I could not find either Vernon or Erol, so I spent the rest of the show bobbing my head in the back and drinking Red Stripes and hitting on the bartender, who wasn't having any of it.

The show ended with a decent encore and me running into the gorgeous Kuwaiti baker girl from my work, a restaurant on the godforsaken Upper East Side of Manhattan. I wondered to myself if she could tell how fucked up I was, and then I wondered to myself why I keep running into temptresses tonight and how I can carry on, like this. Outside the venue, I scoured the crowd for Erol and/or Vernon. I even looked for Sally, and the hot half desert dessert girl from my job. I couldn't find anyone, and Erol was not picking up his cellphone. I must've called him one-hundred-and-sixty-two times while standing outside that place, watching the crowd disperse.

I texted Sally and I texted other girls, like Barbara and Kelly and Nicole and Samantha. I was kinda horny and very drunk. Finally, I gave up and headed for the subway. I did find Vernon sitting by himself on a bench, waiting for the L train. We high-fived but didn't talk, I could tell he was fucked, so I asked him if he had seen Erol, he hadn't, and then I asked him if he had any blow left, he did. He handed me the big bag and said, "Here, if I do anymore I am going to have a goddamn heart attack and die." I did a little nip-nip right there in the subway station and told Vernon to text me when he got to his place as to let me know he got home okay. He nodded and stumbled onto the dead-end Brooklyn-bound train. My train came soon, too, and, low and behold, it was full of uniformed police officers and I kept thinking about the big bag of cocaine in my front right pocket. I got out at Union Square and got on the Uptown 6 train. They all got out at Union Square and they all got on the Uptown 6 train. Were they on to me?

The cops got off at Grand Central, thank god, and I got off at 86th street. I went to the corner store and bought a forty and sat on my stoop and tried to come down from the coke. Just when I was about to go inside, my left front pocket vibrated, scaring me out of my jeans. I thought, for a second, it might be Sally.
It was Erol calling me from his place; he sounded absolutely wasted, saying that he left at the start of the second song and got into a cab, and vomited on the floor of said cab, and now he was home, in his bed, with a bucket next to his head. I finished my beer and went inside and went to sleep, for I had to work at the restaurant tomorrow.

That Spring Concussion for Nothing for Something

I was at a pub in the North
and some cunt walked in
talking shit about Americans,
specially Black Americans.
He said the word Nigger
one too many times.
I was drunk and I punched him in the head,
knocking him off his pedestal.
I stood over him and kicked him twice
and called him the Nigger once.
His mates hit me from behind
with a chair and I was arrested the bigot.
No Italy that spring,
just a night in jail and a concussion.

Where is 12?

Newness and air.
When we fall
Oh when we fall
We cause seasons to change.

Waiting to hear
Oh waiting for the hour
Right after eleven o'clock
We show our fangs.

Keep me awake
In the palm of your hand
In the red sheets of your bed
In the hair falling from your head
And into my face.
It smells like a girl's hair should,
It smells so good.

Keep me awake
In the ghost of the noon,
In the blowing red curtains
In the fading light that comes through,
wrapped in your naked legs
so I can't get away.

But oh baby I can be a lion's soundview
for at least a week
knowing these drinking holes
are dangerous reminders.

He Died with 143.27 Dollars

if he wasn't dead already,
this would make a great song title.
he was from Huntington, West Virginia,
originally.

it has been two years
since he combed his hair, alive.

her name was Angie,
it still is Angie.

she knows the mornings
and the reasons why.

he was an artist and a writer,
and a Golden State Warriors fan.

suicide wasn't an option,
not like cocaine and rockandroll.

his mother was Japanese,
she had to bury her eldest son.

for Mashed Potato Johnson,
life was short and congenial.

busstops and chaperones, disqualifications, too...
the month was April, the day does not matter.

I was always close to tears
for what was said about him.

but I was always intrigued, and often baffled,
about what was not said about him.

what did his tattoos mean,
and how much money was in his Montreal bank
account?

Poem

damn you,
eternal fate!

just have me stabbed
before I get where I'm going.

Sporadic

Spontaneous.
Gravity.
Two.
Four.
Can't.
Change.
Fate.
Shit.
Meet.
Me.
Somewhere.

The.
Electrician.
The.
Evil.
Birds.
The.
Airports.
One.
Three.
Can't.
Change.
Fate.

The.
Old.
Picket.
Fence.

Don't.
Get.
Caught.
Watching.
The.

Paint.
Dry.

Sporadic, indeend.

Patchy.
Random.
Erratic.
Oklahoma.
Love.
Like.
Last.
Year.
Death.
With.
Names.
And.
Nouns.
Nothing.
Else.
We.
Feel.
Forbidden.
For.
As.
Long.
As.
We.
Live.

My.
Name.
Is.
Great.

My.
Life.

Is.
Periodic.

Poem, Mix CD 888

26. *Winter Song* by The Head and The Heart
27. *Misery* by Gallows
28. *Hands Reversed* by Tokyo Police Club
29. *Everything Zen* by Bush
30. *Donald and Lydia* by John Prine

After All

Night boys buy laughter
in green shoes.
Their lips have been chapped
since the winter of 1996.

"Check out this Murphy!"
the damned Mexican said.
His high-pitched voice,
all nose,
hurt my hung-over head.

Vomiting was inevitable.
Three by me,
a knife ride,
pissing in a canoe.

I let go
for girl
in yellow wife-beater
and black bra.

Missed my chance
by half a sucker punch
to the back of the brain,
this is an old letter to you.

Hold on,
Oxford Cleric,
I promise to bleed
for you.

I have never been anywhere.
Except here.

Baby, there's an old

Madison in front of
me in the rain
holding appeal.

Less parenting about Texastown,
more murder from above,
I know I am just a dump truck,
but atleast I've been in love.

Art the very least,
meet me for a drink in the East
where I killed a bald eagle
out of allegory spite.

A beer.
A shot.
A Long Island Iced Tea,
and the looming possibilities.

The Overheards of the Shepherd's Pie Night

of the sky,
nothing is over...

let's celebrate this fact
with two eighty seven,
while Matt English is at work,
and I urge Chris to email that chick
via messy text messages,
and Vernon is nowhere to be found.

nickels are everywhere
and I see another dead bird.
Wednesday, I saw one
in midtown, around seven.

trying in vein to accidentally run into Earlier heaven...

however, no more howl of derision,
can't say no on stage.
eat the peas anyway
and damn is the whole
thing damn delicious!
wait. just. wait.

do you recall the days
with the trains?
the ones that didn't involve worry
or mirrors
or forty-one minutes;
silverware and longing,
punk rock and feeling young again, again.

wardrobe change,
and a savior in paperback human skins...

I had forgotten all about that
book with the green dinosaurs,
until the memory hit me like spite,
with visions of delicious death,
while I finished unpacking.

grab anything to be overheard...

"For what it's worth, I love you..."
he said into a cellphone on N. Henry in Brooklyn.
"But," then he continued.
"Beautiful women have lost
their _____ (fill in the blank, because this word was
inaudible)
in my eyes!"

the overheards,
like the dead bird,
steal my confidence
like a hurricane,
as it was,
and as it were,
I was just a wordsmith
and I slightly died
in the storm.

people only hear what they want to hear...

I hear a hospice.
I hear a home-cooked meal.

Ramble

I do not mind
the justice
or the mice
or the construction
of the 2nd Avenue Subway
and the subsequent noise.

I do not mind
the booze
or the Jeff Goldblum movies
or the weird smell
in the new hallway.

I certainly do not mind
the photographs.

Those.

I do, however,
mind the big deals
and the canceled youth,
but I do not mind
the tears
or the sleepy kissy
mornings,
they both taste so good.

I do not mind
licking them both
up to the max of the sky,
disdained,
full,
snuggled and juggled
by lips and convictions,
after which,

I do not mind
falling to my doom.

P is for Patience

I. *Tonight*

I needed weird poetry tonight.
Another open mic.
I needed to be alone tonight.
So I know.
I don't want to be alone tomorrow night.
When you read these words.
I want you to scream them.
Remind me I am real.
My friend Tom swears hope is a currency.
I believe him.
And then I accidentally cut my pinky finger.

II. *ep. nine six*

They rocknroll.
Yo entiendo.
Landlords burn.
Boxes, too.

Proof is fire-proof.
This poem is proof.

Let's not ruin everything.

Mystery is mysterious.
Years are seconds.
In The Middle of metaphors.
Somewhere.

One day I will tell you.
Over wine.
And under fireworks.

Pull yourself apart.
Arms first.
I have arms.
The rest is history.

III. *Ghosts in Ghosts*

I shake so sorry for living.
I shake violently.
I hear voices that are not Spanish anymore.
I ruined yesterland with whiskey.
Something that ends sentences started at seven in the
dawn.
I am not a king.
I am not strong.
I am a river.
Sometimes.
Something that calls and hangs up happy at two into
midnight.
I hate this poem.
I set my eyes on autopilot.
I shake so violently for living.

IV. *BLUE, TOO*

Everything to everyone.

Crocodiles are better than the future.

According to my bank account.
And last night's prank phone calls.
I am a failure.

I love amongst lightning strikes.
I sing on the edge, out of time.

The world is gonna end.

And I am gonna be stuck at work.

I think I need eye glasses.

Let's repent.
Let's run.
Let's eat ice cream.
Let's go swimming.

Yours

Liaise with sound.

Once upon a yeartime,
I cried a lake.

It was then, when I was lonesomeness
with dears and an audience.

Neck of the woods,
three hundred hangovers that year.

No rocks or salt or nails
when I was not yours.

I was going to seek out and kill
whomever thought brunch was apt
punishment for everyone involved.

Summer was nothing but April
and April was nothing
but the sound of lakes.

I did nothing
when I was not yours.

Willytowne

Meet me at The Lovin' Cup!

I'll take the L train from Union Square
and you will walk from your place in Greenpoint.

We'll drink whiskey before the show.

You be prim,
I'll be the asshole.
I'll break your heart,
you break mine.

Oh, so young and fast,
almost thirty years
for us to find this place,
here and here and here.

Found the mustache manifesto
mixed in with long division
in my wallet with an old bag of cocaine.

I like the part where you Call me a liar.
It's the only truth
in the whole 'I don't love you anymore' lie.

Montreal has my money.
My house is made of water.
And if you want to love me, you just will.

Again and again and.
Again.

Pen a farewell poem about transience.
Tonight.
And about unobtainable love.

I will be so tired tomorrow
as I pick up bullets tonight
in Willytowne,
with my teeth,
just east
of the endless adoration and endless doubt.

Needle in a Haystack

the July night
was cooler than most
and Vernon had a shallow spot
adjacent to the symphony;
it was there under pine trees
with mosquito spray and skateboards;

late was I with my spite and blues,
my afterwork doldrums and lovelorn nine-beers-deep.

the music in the grass
and the old dead pine needles,
dummy patience and the shadows of the trees,
there are too many for you to see me.

to the night, come find me,
darling, come closer.

my knees know not where to lead
and the swan was not getting back to me
or my goddamn pathetic text messages;
this is just a Tuesday fantasy.

then,
fate got interesting,
hysterics follow me
in a cab to Penn Station
as fast as fast can be
as I have poeticated before:
as good as good goes.

my hands and heart out of control
then in the crowd of seas,
the violas started too,
and I saw you,

under the sad marquee,
where the cold desire grew so much brighter.

I couldn't believe my eyes I found her,

you,
darling,
the scientific beautiful.

Midnight at Biddy's Pub

Couldn't sleep through the Manhattan sweating
summer
of fear of dissolution of take-me-to-the-table-and-kill-
me,
so I woke up and found old poems from ten summers
ago,
and reasoned with myself to get up and leave the
Spanish house,
and walk to Biddy's Pub at midnight on the corner of
Unity and Forgotten:
come one and only one and dance with me on the M
train to Taiwan.

Gh'oweihfoisdh

new smells
remind me of old smells
and 101st street never looked so pretty
with its wet joy and affliction.

Remember getting a chance?
I remember train rides
at night.
Listening to *The Fleet Foxes.*

Remember Arms?

I was in the middle of it all
and I cut my arms off
instead of making decision(s).
I don't look into mirrors any more.

Goddamn it all to Halloween Hell.

new poem
about poetry
and hate.

that's a good start.

I built these walls that you call your own.

I.
Subway.
Dirty.
Instead.

secretly going through a silent hurricane.

cocaine.

panda.
wallets.
molestors.
Biddy's Pub.

Awful arguments.
Alone.
and six months to live.
cigarette.
ashes.
and phone calls.
and midnights, too.

I've forgotten
what it's like
to be a ghost
and the scariest
day
is
Kick-on Tuesday
for me.

I stop breathing.

Uniquely.
Free.
Lightning bugs in Union Square.
The night I cut my hair.

that's a good start.
to a day of the dead.
July 1st,
2010.

There

There is a stage.
With violas, surely.
The summer night.
Not as hot as the night before.

There is something.
To be said.
For patience.
And not giving up.

There is a smile.
And a note.
While port-o.
Red velvet cupcakes.

There is more.
Proof, doubtless.
And fireworks.
A dancing kid.

Buck

I found a hundred dollar bill
on the street on the day of the desert,
as an act of congress
declared popwar heat.

No, I didn't tell my few friends,
I bought booze
and concert tickets
and took her name in vain.

And then I gave
sixty-five dollars
and change
to a hobo on Leonard Street.

Future Poetry

The time machine
in my backyard
sits unused,
rusting in the rain,
because it was
an impulse buy,
and our mom's always warned
us against impulse buys,
and after reading the manual
and taking it on a few test-runs,
I have grown terrified
of its possibilities

I didn't see when I was going to die
but I saw how, which, by the way,
has made me never want to ride a bike again.

I saw nothing in the past
that made me smile,
and nothing in the future that made me want to say
more.

That's it!
I have to burn the time machine.

Are there others?

Shit.
I have to burn the others!
And kill the scientists.
And destroy their lab notes.

But first I want to take it for one more spin.

Poem

Stay baby stay!
I know I am crazy,
but I love the way
you say, "Go to hell!"

Blood Blisters

The song stops.

We scrape and scratch
with our feet,

corners of pages,

with chrome spots
on our beer bottles,
and this is what she said.

"Bleed and Live, Ryan *fucking* Buynak!"

Cars outta this place.

Tears on a face.

I do not want to be brave.
I want to be bold.

Like

like gorgeous
with
like big brown eyes
set deep in the skull
and like
these dimples.
oh my god
you are like gorgeous
something like a boy's dream
with
like amazing
everything
larger than life
like sinew
and belief,
like drugs
like love.

Slap the Bell

We only listen to our dreams when they tell us what we
want to hear.
We only kid around when we were kids.
We only drop to our knees to service someone.
We only fall in love when it is impossible.

Tetanus

swell days of everything...

Clock out of the restaurant,
summer nights are on their way out.

It's 11:10.
Brooklyn is consistency.
Greenpoint.
Morgan Ave.
Vinny's pizza place.

The subway from Graham.
Speech that is new.
Skateboards...and cute puppies, goddamn it.
The L into Manhattan.
Everymorning, everymorning.

Shit and wash face.
In a rented bathroom.
Somewhere in Spanish Harlem.
Afternoon stoops.
Afternoon drunken stupors.
Wasted days on the Westside.

75th and Columbus.
Beers and blow.
Erol and his bratty work friends.
Ignorance is bliss.
Especially in the midst of inopportune importance.
Blind eyes on the 1 Line.
All the way down to the Bowery Ballroom.

Memories are mine.
These.
Skinny Love.

This place, a lovetime ago.
Bummed cigarettes on Delancey.
And that's it.
Skips a beat.
Spun around.

Run to Union Square.
Sit on a bench.
The Bench.
Wish for more wishes.
It's 11:11pm.
Remember everykiss, everynight.
I walk down to the Rumbler.
Take the G to Nassau.
Cut my hand on a sharp stanchion.

Passive harassment.
In the form of silent following.
Upstairs.
She says she can find someone else to love her.
Midnight.
The Love Making.
Morning.
Found drugs.
The Fear.
Knock on a red frontdoor and remembering
everylittlethingfromlastyear.

It's 11:12pm.

Sharp Guns and Semi-Automatic Knives

loser...

what a nice testimony.

I know the life I lead.
I know my enemies.

Villains aren't happy with their decisions,
they are just scared...

it's like shaking a can of pennies at a dog.

Pride?
what the fuck is that like?
who sold me this anger?
I bartered for it.

there is no place to land,
interesting kismet...
for what it is worth, like the last poem in the book,
this is not the end.

Long division.
Remember east.
Gold as hell.
I spit on people there.

And set myself on fire,
be it twelve...
avenge my one-and-only,
skinny lips,
making peace with neck.

I am not the moon.
I am a quitter.

117

I have died twelve and a half times.
I say half because I haven't fully died
from this last time.

First-best, I know.

The Killroy Days

I live in a rented room
somewhere in the past,
where good things come
and go so fast.

My T face,
sore and sored,
from slapping the bell,
from squinting
into the setting sun,
yesterland,
and the rising sun
just hours ago
as we climbed
the Queens Borough Bridge.

Decisions
be
death
on this continent.

I am not in Miami Beach nigh.

Killed myself twice in California.
Never been to Oklahoma.
Mexico City girly poets bedazzle me
before noon, EST, by my black watch.

But,
bullshitted and bitched up,
here, in New York City,
by a lass named Madalyn, who
seems like a good girl
who needs a good ugly cry,
because she is beautiful

all of the time.

and why is it that
beautiful single girls
always own puppies,
and those puppies
are almost always Yorkshire Terriers?

I wonder if she wonders
where her clouds have gone?

shines too long sometimes, though,
a limerick about sunshine.
She is definitely not dead,
wander away from her days,
text by text, sex by sex.

she will sing.
loud so long ago.
Joyous yester skids,
tall and as happy as tomorrow is unknown.

But she will forget about me.
Eventually.
Indefinitely.
During the year of intersections.
She asked me last night what *Cherish* means.
I told her about treasures.

Thinking of guns,
starring in her irony.
Life can be so fair as it goes along,
tshirts and bracelets
instead of memories.

French kissing.
saw her in San Fran in 2005.

Her eyes.
Gave her away.
Gold as hell.

It's gonna take some very interesting fate to make this
happen,
for what it's worth,
life is short.

Lock and load, Richard, Murphy, etc.

She is whore crimson.
She is over it all.
She is from Long Island and Florida.
She is simultaneously simultaneous.
She is gorgeous.

My knuckles are bleeding,
My birthday is tomorrow and gone.

She lights in lighted nights.

Stretch
and bleed,
do not depend on me.

foldable past.
period.
diligent delusions.
amusement.

I am not strong.

Her lips are tin.
Her eyes are pavement.

It wasn't a dream.

It was confidence.
Finally.
I wish I had said better things.
I wish I were cool.
I am not cool.

Where the Giraffe is Rabid

I think about
death most
in the movie
theater,

especially,
and almost
exclusively,
during despondent
comedies,
like this.

I haven't had a
solid shit
in a month,
haven't jerked off
in two,
haven't slept through a night in who knows how long.

Life ain't too easy for a fool like me.

I bought a desk,
she bought a new dress.

I am not good at anything,
except falling in love,
and writing.

I am pretty good at air hockey.

I am severely addicted to tin
and Somewhere.
I used to see the night so anxious.

Subsequently, I was defeated by the Death Wish

or the Death Bridge, depending on where you are from
and that place's fads.

In: Misanthropy.
Out: Psychotic Whores.

Last night was the end.
I thought we both understood this fact.

The Axe

"Be tall," she said.
"And be youthful. You are not *you* when you feel old.
and you have been looking and feeling old lately."

I was 28.
She was right.

I had a grand in the bank, maybe.
I had forty dollars from 2004 in a bank in Montreal.
My breakfast consisted of eggs and tin and chicken feet
and whiskey and loathing and love.

I got arrested in Miami last month.
No criminal charges.
Little blow.

When I was a kid,
with paper and crayons,
I always colored outside of the lines,
but not on purpose.

I held my pencils and crayons differently than the
other kids.
They noticed this more than my lisp or my birthmark.

"You'll find someone else to take care of you," she said.
She was right.

"You'll fall in love with some other stupid girl," she
said. She was wrong.

When I was a kid,
with rattail lice,
I always had little lies
hidden under my skin.

I made up stories, because...well, because I could.
Now I call myself a writer.

"I'm tired of the loveless letdowns," she said. "And the
goddamn lies!"

We were alone in a laundry mat.
We had been drinking red.
We folded undies.
We heckled over ardor and its doldrums.
I bit my tongue mostly.
It wasn't my turn to be upset.
It wasn't my turn to tell my story.

I thought of childhood, mine in general.

And I thought about the fact
that my maternal grandmother died while doing
laundry.

Paperboy

When I was a stupid kid,
for some cinematic reason,
I always wanted to be a paperboy.

The position held certain
romance in my mind,
mixed with a sense of community
that was never there.

I wanted the Orlando Sentinel
to notice my bike talents.
I wanted responsibility
and to peddle past neighbors
with their smiles and cups of coffee.
Miriam would be in a robe
with her kids getting on a school bus.
Gay Glen would be walking his german short-haired
pointer.

block by block.

instead, I cut lawns
to help my mom pay the rent...
which turned out to be addictions.

Dominico Street,
and Chickadee Avenue.

Ignored by harbors,
I weed-whacked.

my older brother
bought a Nissan
with drug money,
my grandmother died.

winter means only
more summer,
back then in Florida,
and I just wanted to ride
my Huffy,
and throw newspapers at front porches.

Poem, Mix CD 888

6. *Golden Brown* by The Stranglers
7. *Treatment Bound* by The Replacements
8. *All My Days* by Alexi Murdoch
9. *Clarity* by John Mayer
10. *The City* by The Glorious Veins

Central Florida Yesterdays

the
Colonial Promenade, long ago,
had rhymes,
laughter and losers, like us.

(407) area code.
247-8452 everywhere.

now,
new hat.
new girl.

everything I cherish is slowing dying
or
is gone.

from California to New York
back to Florida,
and back in time,
hope in telephones and written on bathroom walls.

Best buddy,
Casselberry and pictures,
tell the past I said hi and
that I am okay.

And on a day
when Winter Park
will open up
who will I call,
besides the insects?

I always picture it as an apocalyptic wasteland.

Anathema

steak and potatoes
and sacrifice
and
goddamn poetic saturday night...

some studio in Midtown.
a collective.
the venue was fine.
the drunkards were standing in the back.
the druggies were hamming it up in the lobby.
the socialists were sitting on the floor right up front.
Kerouac would have been proud.

she never did show.
so I bought blow from Charlie.
I liked Charlie's poems and he read them well.
then my name was called.
I stepped over the socialists.
I read some new ones.
One, I dedicated to Charlie, for the blow.
I owe him twenty bucks, now.
One I dedicated to her, Somewhere.

Charlie and I got the fuck out of there
when the open mic resumed.
We walked sixty blocks, give or take.

our mouths moved to silly poems about Times Square
and the pretentiousness of heartbreak,
how its hurt is relative to the suicide dreamer.
I left Charlie at 96th.
Saw a Puppet on the bus reading an old copy of *Leaves
of Grass*.
Kerouac would have been proud.

watching the weekends die
was something so grand, a sport.
these days were made of paper,
and I ripped them to shreds.

Rolled up dollar bills are an awful poem.
Inebriated textmessages to Witchita.
Ancient East River, and I have no fear for only a few
minutes of the day
most of which come when I am asleep.
The best part is necks at 2:42 am.

Home, a home, an apartment, I call it mine,
I sit at the typer and hammer out an outline,
which turns into a bitter sync of rollercoasters,
these nights I call mine too,
most of which I share with one million strangers,
in one hundred million windows.
Bushwick Blues by Delta Spirit comes on the RyPod.
I open a beer and the next thing I know,
the shy sun is reading over my shoulder.

I have to get ready for work.
I am the king of contradictions and double standards.
I am a popculture casualty.
I plowed through the day as best I could.
The Mexicans in the back of the house
knew the shape I was in and they made me good food.
I did the remainder of the white,
just to get me halfway towards another night.

after work, the afternoon,
Avery called and said he was at Luke's apartment.

poetic saturday has morphed through the clock of
employ,
and has turned into Yacht Rock Sunday.

132

Luke's place was on 73rd and 1st.
I hated seven flights of stairs.
When Luke opened the door,
Avery was in the background making awful noises.
I walked into the bedroom
and saw Avery on his knees servicing a mirror with
lines of white powder.

Luke put on some Steely Dan.
We laughed out loud.
Born to die.
Luke worked with Avery at the tv channel.
I liked Luke, he was fucking funny,
but not goofy, just cleverly funny.
And apparently, his girlfriend left for Spain
and had to leave behind a substantial amount of white.

I got a textmessage from Witchita.
It said 'Give me hope for the night and promise you love
me.'

I promised the end.

Percentage Poem

49 percent
of the night
is spent in bars
and 16 percent is spent
on stoops,
while Dan
sings me poetry
and stupid girls with French
Bulldogs walk past
and what happens
to the other 35 percent,
no one knows.

Kansas

Cardinal water.
Fixed water.
Dearth.

Pilot Therapy.

Sturdy silos between Leavenworth and Atchison,
those pillars represent *the* September.

The other album.
The first song.

She was famous
since borne
into my corner
of the world.

Her focus three days gone.

The winter we got married
was in Kansas right after August.

I wish I would've listened to my sister when she tried to
teach me about love.

I know by rote
that this is what it is
and that this is what it
is supposed to be.

It's okay to feel a little strange in Kansas,
because
plagiarized textmessages say it all:

I want to love you exponentially.

It's already begun.
Please don't stop me.
And listen to what I have to say.
I am going to say a whole lot.
Because there's a lot to gain.
Or a lot to lose.
And I'm not here to lose.

On Bleecker

Vernon was the one who already perished.
Erol was the one who was already saved.
I was the one who spent all these eagles.
        as flickering time wrecked all of our
hopelessness.

In between MacDougal and Sullivan.
Falling in love in funny hats.
The sun has melted in half, hours ago,
        and this coyote creek just so happens to be
concrete.

Hands of glory, of Manhattan.
Three hundred hangovers that year.
The foul year of forever, dense 2009,
        when we were all running through lawns with
boiled spines.

Everywhere at once, we are.
We are the goddamned Hipster Generation.
We forget the fools who gave their punkrock lives for
us,
        but we booze with the best of them, just
translation of years.

America

'Tis a great Monday to explode
into a million bits,
because America still exists,
trust me.

In between bathwater and car wrecks,
there are coyotes and girls and everything.

Hearts are in stomachs, I see and feel with fists,
and awful people serfdom me,
and Hollywood is just a place
that calls me names aimlessly uncool.

In between Love and Christmas,
the fur of the fox,
and American Lies,
lies, lies...lies a child.

In between St. Augustine, Fl.
and Atchison, KS,
the divorcees buy birds and coffee,
and pray, prey, pry windows open.

Honey, come home
carrying a tomahawk
and let us buy a house with a fixed mortgage,
in Colorado, with a red door.

Find that thing we really need,
as the red, setting sun
falls so hard
on the Pacific Ocean.

Without which
we couldn't be,

Abraham Lincoln would laugh,
the ghosts are ghosts.

Will-Power and Power Bills

Most folks,
unfortunate or not,
some in the middle,
like me,
wake up every day
and say to themselves
that this is the day
that I am going to change my life...

and by the afternoon it is raining
and that dream is overshadowed
by work and wear
and drugs and love.

I want to tell the world
that there is a really good reason
I am the way that I am
but I can't think of a good excuse.

I want to walk out of my kitchen,
through the side door,
and walk away from this place
and leave the electric bill
unpaid on the counter
and the fish still swimming
in its bowl.

Again,
I don't need to be brave,
I want to be bold.
Regret is a disorder of the nervous system
and wasting days is an art.

Drawing a Picture of the Sound of Her Smiling

sometimes you forgive people
because you want them in your life...

it's sticky in here,
with sticky arms, bare,
and watered eyes
that glow no matter what
the story the mouth is telling.

the nose fulminates,
there is no ennui
inside,
ever,
and this makes me jealous
of the verve, the life writ large
and showing up over sad sandwiches.

there are crumbs at the corners,
but trust me,
it adds to the perfection,
as if Frankensteined and made for Mercedez to sell
to the west.

I have to catch my breath.

Those wonderful lips
should not be mine,
God sees to this in some sad scientific karma,
and before I know it,
she is frowning over sad salads
and I have seen this face before,
my only crime.

It's tough being the liar
over coffees and cigarettes,

but there is only one truth:

My shoulders shake while
She is the most beautiful
woman in the wide world.

I won't let the wide world forget this fact.
I will draw a picture, I say aloud!

Then, I wipe boogers on my pants.
I shiver,
because I stole her happiness.

I won't let this end with a ticket and a broken door.
Her teeth are as white as the truth of dice.

And so I sketch,
drunk from memory,
with charcoal and blood:

the edges of existence.

Sweating and Pissing and Dying

Brown David and Matt English
are great at what they do.
They are the best Spanish rock act
and they, bless their hearts,
fed me blow for hours.

And that means that tonight's poetry
is going to be awesome only for tonight
and tomorrow's punching the clock
is gonna suck for them
and also Country Luke, who danced the night away
despite being the only one on the dance floor.

And I am in trouble because I am out of money
and I don't work tomorrow.
Waiting tables is like fishing for endangered species,
and we all fish here in these parts of Manhattan.
And I am in trouble because the lady caught me in a lie.

And I forget the point of this poem:

Vernon was sweating.
I was pissing.
Matt English was dying.

Witnesses to mornings
after staying up all night,
gigging and drugging,
now in need of covers and caring women,
we make our way home, respectively.

Vernon goes to Harlem.
I go to Kansas.
Matt English goes to hell
and looks for heat and hospice

and dead birds.
We all look for dead birds.
Brown David followed his own heart..
He lives on and plays the viola
in West Hollywood.
while three of us watch the sun rise from better days.

Vernon is a wannbe.
Matt English is the real thing.
Brown David is dead in 2012.
I am on a poet's mission,
but I forget everything.

Poem

Thank the liars.
For lying.
Indeed.

When folks and fuckers
don't hide shit,
it means they don't care
about losing your soul.
Forever.

Written Over

'Tis raining right now in New York City,
a damn good excuse not to go out into the world today,
but, low and behold, I got shit to do,
and so I venture into it, the world, without umbrella;
umbrellas are for suckers,
it would just keep my head dry
and turn inside with the wind.

I squint to the post office
and the line is short due to the rain,
but there are twelve open clerks.
Why is it that when this hellhole is full of queues
there are only ever two employees working the
registers, and when there are only two customers, like
now, there are a dozen mail clerks?
Universal law, I guess.

The rain picks up,
I duck into a coffee shop
and ask for beer.
The brown dude shakes his head and just walks away.
Skip the coffee,
I know how he feels,
like the world will end
while he is punching the clock.

Fuck it, I mumble,
as I bow to the thunder overhead,
a warning, doubtless,
to disappear, which I do so well.

Sorry, I say, to the day,
and then I go to the bank with business
that could've been handled on the internet,

but paranoia is king here, especially in my broken ribs.
I walk out of my way to a branch
where they know my name.
Madison Avenue, I am probably the only long-hair
who ever walks in here.
Devine, the bank man, and I always talk basketball
and today we curse LeBron for not coming to the
Knicks. Devine always calls me Mr. Buynak,
no one has ever called me Mr. Buynak.
I deposit one hundred and forty dollars.

Upon crossing 88th street,
a truck catches a puddle just right
and soaks me from the waste down.
I laugh with strangers and figure I deserved something
like that. Hard luck, and until next kick-on Tuesday, I
don't give a fuck about anything.
I drop off some books at The Corner Bookstore,
for some reason they like my stuff, and they move it.
While inside, I catch a cold, and send a text message to
someone saying 'Don't Ever Give Up.'

On my walk back to my waterless room, uphill, my
shoes make slopping sounds, I pick up a copy of the
Times and a bottle of Johnny Walker Red. It is time to
read and shit and write; they are all the same thing,
anyways. Like unobtainable love and/or death…all
unused Lighthouses.

Once inside, I don't do anything with the lights,
put my keys down and HI to Una, the old lady,
who may or may not be a ghost that only I can see.
I suddenly remember that I have a poetry gig this
evening deep into goddamn Brooklyn, and then I notice
a singular solitary silent second, rare in New York.
Then I hear the Rumbler shaking the building from
below. It is an Uptown Local, I bet, and that is what I

147

started with, a story about some dude, lost like me,
good at life, but not great, and he is riding the
subway...somewhere.

The typewriter is a symphony...sometimes.

South is Relative

Powders and pills
in the corner unchanged,
she is young and famous.

The bourbon is gone,
her mom drank it all
while I was east.

Brazil sees me.
Canada sees me.
I bought a used Lexus with a Ghost in it.

It was a good day still.
It was today.
Fourteen hundred and sixty days ago.

I lost my brother
to bullets and Brooklyn.
He used to carry me home.

Fire Escape

He enters his two-bedroom apartment.
He takes in his breath and thinks about his first person point-of-view,
tired as the King of Algeria.
He sits for a minute on a second-hand ottoman, after work.
He is tired from his postal minions.
He is tired from his terrorized times.
He is young but feels old. He coughs.
He is of the haiku working poor.

His roommate enters and says a casual hello.
He gets up and goes from couch to room.
Window south.
Manhattan mountains.
Talks to roommate through walls.
Yells about Bills.
Packs a bowl of marijuana.
Goes out onto the fire escape.

He has shaky legs out here.
His brown hair is blowing.
He smells rain.
Eventually it rains. He stays out.
He takes in his breath and thinks of freedom and infant springtime.
He touches strings on his wrist.
He pulls a lighter from the back left pocket of his jeans.
Only ever jeans.
He lights an American joint and inhales and curses it all.
He thinks it is all great.
Finally.
He takes in his breath and thinks about free will and the grace of the wanted sky above. This is it.

He thinks these things, working hard,
until he takes a proverbial step back
and sees a window from his point of view.
This window is the back of the building behind his
building.
It was open.
There was a stranger dancing inside.
He could see her ankles.
It, the window, must've been open only three inches, no
more.
No rain, if it had rained in the first hour.
The curtains in said window were opened just about
four inches.
Point of view.
The sun disappeared on him.
His joint went with the wind.
He sat elated at the calm.
He breathed and sang under his breath.
Across the tenement pavilion from him,
a window was open unto a world.
A world of ankles and sweat or water from showers.
These ankles were connected to sweet feet.
They looked like a girl's feet should.
They pounced up and down from time to time,
but for the most part it was nothing but ankles.
One second, he saw a collar bone, but he doesn't know
how or why.

He sits vested with his knuckles on his knees.
He wishes for rain but rain never comes back.
Neither does summer.
The stars barely show themselves.
His eyes' eyelids close on the tarred land.
The day is barely sitting atop the horizon and troubles
are far from gone.

He wants to go inside, but he sees tiny ankles again and
they seem to be two-stepping.

This is when he notices, in the falling dark,
that the existing curtains across from his are glade
green,
they are not new.
They are open as much as they should be.
He takes what he wants from his window point of view,
not a wild hunt. The ankles disappear again.
He is too goddamn tired and uninspired to grace such
things romantic.
Does he still believe as he goes inside and his roommate
says to him the phone is for you? He sinks his
shoulders and hears a ringing in his ears.
He thinks of crimes and why.
He thinks of a stranger's ankles
and what she looks like waking up in the morning in a
big white bed.

His feet feel good in the long awaited autumn.
His socks are off, transplanted from motivation.
He sits on the rusted stairs, snapshots, shitty weed.
Movies are overdue.
This afternoon was longer than most.
He still wears his navy blue shirt.
No stains today.
He finishes his referred refer.
He coughs. He watches the bastard city birds
breeching.
He gets up to go, but he hears music from across the
concrete canyon.
He stands still for four hundred and twenty eight
seconds.
He wants to dance with her.
To pop music. He becomes self-aware.

The curtains across are closed. They are still green. The
window is open a bit of half.
But he hears her music. He stops moving and coughs
and goes back inside for the night.
He gives up on laundry because you can't win in this
world.

As the air cools in New York, for season's want, the
windows open and the music louder.
He sweats out of pride.
His roommate refuses to split the electric bill.
He goes outside onto the fire escape twice a day.
He drinks his coffee out there in the morning.
He smokes his joints out there in the evenings.
His shirt doesn't stick to his back anymore.
He hasn't experienced winter out there yet.
The rusted metal must be cold, not to mention the
window, eight stories high.

Another night, outside, dragging on his picture,
dragging smoke down his throat,
standing on his tippy toes for no reason.
The sky was still red.
His shoulders went back and up when the window
across from his balcony point of view went from dark
green to a lighted bedroom.
The ankles were seen first.
Then the knees, thatched and thin.
The scene was slow motion and somewhat surreal.
Today hadn't been great to him.
He was feeling sorry for himself for a while,
until an unexpected muse stepped outside of her
wayward life
and onto the fire escape and lit a cigarette.

He was stunned. He was immobile.
He was suddenly aware of his every movement.

He was trying to look casual, so casual.

She didn't look like he had expected.

She had the ankles of a blonde, or so he thought. She was a brunette.

She was wearing cut off jean shorts. She was wearing a yellow tank top.

She must be freezing. She might be strong.

He and she caught eyes for two and a half seconds.

Too many beautiful moments.

She sucked on her cigarette and looked at her cellphone.

He pretended not to care.

He was not alright and neither was she.

Nights begin and end.

Most prior to the blink of an eight hour shirt.

Summers come and go.

Gone.

The curtains changed.

One coffee morning they were not green anyone.

Now they were a pattern of red squares and bolts.

He smoked the last of his weed and flicked the roach down into the canyon.

He had never seen anyone down there.

He did the work at opening an old window and went back inside one foot at a time.

His roommate was walking around without a shirt.

His concave chest was now in a video game battle.

The Sunday was over.

So was the season.

Her Bookshelf

the teeny-tiny paper star
fell from the ceiling
and landed on my black shoe,
the right one of the two.

I picked it up
and put it in this teeny-tiny
notebook to save forever
or until some deathly fire,
like a movie ticket stub.

I looked up,
and forward forever
and focused on the spines in the paper skeletons,
amongst the sturdy steel that has stood here for years,
as the background for her growing black daughter.

I see Kerouac
and the complete Poe and Sherwood Anderson
and my own first book of poems
which is placed outside the file,
facing the inverted room for all the world to see.

I am honored and happy as a child,
whose only wish has come true,
for I am up there on top of that metal shelf
like a monument in her life,
with Jung and Pinecones and stacks of old boardgames,
and pictures of her daughter.

Poem

...he walks around in barefoot goodbyes.
Midnights happen.

Colours

let me say,
liberty is a rare thing...

red ink writes this initially on tiny pages of tiny
notebooks,
while red rain falls outside and runs mascara and rusts
fire escapes.
green shoes, mine, soak and slop uptown,
like red prophecies told by olde red ghosts with pink
nipples seen through naughty nightgowns.
tell white lies in moonlight through
yellow teeth and yellow fear, shaking during
blue balls and blue phonecalls,
and opened grey windows with streaming blue wind
while sitting on white window sills.

blue door, red door,
orange spiral staircase,
blue jeans, brown hair, beautiful eyes.
peach-colored door,
peach sheets, peach pie,
red rain night, drunk fight,
bad breath, bad textmessages from yellow cab.
the colours of freedom
are red and green and yellow,
and black, and blue,
and grey and peach and orange.

Selfish

I will live forever.

Mondays are mine.

Nothing, not even once
did I see *the Light* or Stop Signs.

Imagination for now,
manda bala,
I'm a lonely man
with five bottles
of whiskey,
none to share.

Precisely cocaine
and it is more than me
to be this way.

From the Post Office
to the Liquor Store,
I sing sing sing
a song of myself
and there is ink
in my beard.

I'm thinking about bullets, only,
and maybe catalysts.

The world
is a wonderful place
only on weekends
and I am a Monday man!

Drunk, Leaving Cleveland

I am drunk in Cleveland
and my cellphone ain't workin'.
Poetry barely pays the bills
and these words make me remember
her words spoken so softly
in morning gardens,
in hell,
on Mondays just like tomorrow.

I used to wake up
next to ya
every morning
of that distinguished,
disgusting summer
in Greenpoint, Brooklyn.

I hate when the backs
of my shoes walk on
my dirty denims.

My shoulders are big
and sweaty.
Chris Corso is changing his telephone
number in Orlando, Fl.

LeBron James is gone.
I cut my thumb and now I am using my yellow shirt
as a bandage.

I woke up early
this morning and
I wanted to write
about what we went through,
but I did not want to miss
the Continental Breakfast.

And I don't want to think of her.

I need coffee.
I am glad my cellphone was disabled.
Memories of Kansas City in this morning.
The internet says it is raining there now.
I give myself to the world.
Taiwan later today.
Drunk in Cleveland last night,
where children and dogs play,
today,
whiskeytown,
special,
and eggs.

There is a drunk-and-fat
and-fat-and-drunk
woman on the corner
of an overcast city
wearing a skirt
and I am a lonely
man
heading for the terrible airport
kissing Cleveland goodbye,
and afternoon is debauchery.
Drunk for the last time,
here,
on W. Huron Road.

Today Has Turned From Beauty

to grey with you, Sky!
Said I.

I am an hour and a half
late for work,
I don't care anymore,
and in that hour and a half
I am in a terrible mood
but I do not know
why, exactly,
aside from the smells of the savages and sewers and
south nicks,
strewn about the sidewalk, weekly.

I gave an old lady the finger
for absolutely no reason at all
while she was walking her German Short-Haired
Pointer.
I gave a baby the finger while it was
being pushed in a stroller
by its Mother,
I don't know if it was a boy or a girl.

Subsequently, also, I spit on a jogger
but that was an accident, I promise.
She ran by silently
at the wrong time,
wrong place.
Saliva splash!

Daniel is napping
and I am alone, walking until out of breath.
And
so I drink on the stoop
and write shitty love poems

in a red notebook
while waiting for a response
from the Gods of the cellphones.

I smell the rain a-comin'.
I hope she is ok,
somewhere.
Now I know why the terrible mood
flooded me coldly,
today is the beginning of October,
and my best friends
hold on to strings,
confessional things,
and the walls' messages
have changed.

I am the painter that remains
with only words
with which to work.

My sweety honey pie
has taken me into her arms
and given my a night or two
that I am not soon
to forget;
that was a month ago.

So, dear, what will I do now?

I will move somewhere,
like Kansas City, a loft,
a place the ocean will never see,
a place my friends will only live on pages.

I will be the holy ghost.

LaPlace's Demon

What are thoughts?
Where do they come from?
Poems are only themselves
wonderful thoughts I
do not wish to forget.
Memories are thoughts.
Determinism? Maybe.
I can see what matters,
but what am I seeing,
and where does it come from?
From some sort of shadowworld.
Is it real?
Is it me?

Your Father's Funeral

Weep with me, my dear,
on a train,
on our way
to your father's funeral.

Show me signs
of anger,
of remorse,
of anything.

Don't smile anymore,
even though the rain
has gone away,
it is not appropriate at this venue.

You are not a lion,
neither am I,
deny, my dear,
you mustn't.

Poem

It's still burning,
my collar...

While I try desperately
to get the bartender's attention.
I need a beer.
And she needs a buck.
But I can see she hates me,
as she shakes a martini.
Maybe it is my long hair.
Maybe it is the mustache.
I hate her for hating me.
I was gonna say I'd fuck her,
but now she can go fuck herself.

...I'll take a Red Stripe, I say.
Seven bucks, she says.

The Pilots

One hundred
and ninety
Pilots die
in my hands
and I can't do
a goddamn thing.

They are eaten
by wolves
and sad songs are sung
about said pilots
with car parts in their
fading hair,
always drinking
always far from home.

Let the seasons
begin
with all that
woefully
rattles
in horse bellies,
comparative to coyote snacks
and both of their four keen eyes.

They,
unlike cobras,
and coyotes
and stream-traveling unicorns,
the wayward pilots,
bigots and perverts,
all of them
with mothers too
and mustaches
like me and like you.

They didn't want
to kill anyone, dear,
not in the slightest,

The more you smell
the heaven ceiling
from under the stomping of ocean ghosts, gone,
like Amelia Earhart,
and the cooking, smelly souls,
the more you give up your belongings and
your questions.

Poem, Mix CD 888

21. *Fade Into You* by Mazzy Star
22. *Hard Life* by Bonnie "Prince" Billy
23. *Runaway* by Del Shannon
24. *Innocent* by Taylor Swift
25. *The Last Lonely Eagle* by New Riders of the Purple Sage

Mistreated Montreal

I lived short weeks, weak,
in a stone house with a purple door,
just up Rue Sherbrooke
from McGill University.

I had long lost and short won.

I had begun in New York,
spilled down to Carolina,
at first, after heart-wrench, then
spilled up, out of allegory spite.

The doorbell to the place was broken,
and I liked it that way.
My kitchen window was round,
and, on weekday mornings, I watched the students
walking with backpacks
while I did the dishes, every morning.

The dishes piled up,
 night in and night out,
as Michel and I put holes in Mickeys and Molsons and
bottles of cognac,
and bags of blow, all by ourselves, just us,
and sometimes his random, nameless sluts.

Michel came from France in 1996;
he was a pro, my fellow compatriot of malfunction.

I whispered this way north
on a wasted weekend, via train.
That was six weeks ago, November.
My hands feel oh so different here.

I liked winter, chapter two.

I type this on paper
bought from a Quebecois corner store.

It was our misfortune to be born in this time.
I was trying to leave a little more room
for error these days, as well as room
to correct the error(s).

I was supposed to be working on a novel.
I was just drinking a lot and walking a lot.

I met Michel as a passerby to his protest
of Prince Charles with 137 strangers.
He was drinking French brandy
and chanting "Abort la Monarchie"
but I think he was there just to get drunk
and meet girls.

We were instant friends.
Me with my hangover and blues.
He with his notion of dismantling existence,
a lover with his appurtenances.

He also had his easy equipage,
an old unnamed car, but it had a new CD player.
He had his secrets, too, in his furrowed brow,
probably running from something or someone, like me.

He also had a young wife in France,
or so he told me.
His wife was called Marie.
I called his car The Mini Lion.

We would often drive in the rain aimlessly,
just talking about books and music and smoking
cigarettes.

This was our little tradition.
Whenever it started raining we would run out to his car
and just go.

One evening, while we were driving to a party in
Plateau Mont-Royale,
we were listening to some band from Brooklyn
(Michel loved my music and he devoured it),
we were silent ourselves, shaky from the shtootz,
there was a single bolt of lightning, a spiral staircase
from Heaven, a sign.

At said party, everyone I met wanted to know what
New York was like.
I lied with stereotypes, saying it was full of violence and
heartbreak.
Maybe it was only half lies.
Michel introduced me to a gardener called Gracie.
He called me the best writer in the world.
He introduced me as his bestfriend
from New York and then he whispered into my ear,
something along the lines of...
"Practice on your sins."

With a nose full,
and no mass appeal
I talked to Gracie about poetry
and watched as her eyes gave up on me.

She ended up kicking me seven Xanax,
for a Canadian ten,
and then she disappeared,
and I ended up puking on my shoes and vomiting on my
jeans
in the front yard of the party.

I lost Michel at Midnight,

and so I took a minicab
back to the downtown area,
and I found my place filled with nothing but books.

The walls were empty white.
On one of the books,
I found an old bag of blow.
The Book was *Winesburg, Ohio* by Sherwood Anderson
and I remembered my brother's rule:
Never by blow from brown folks,
which I did, yesterday afternoon
from a dude on the corner of Metcalfe and
Maisonneuve...
And never do blow by yourself
which I proceeded to do.

Bad things happen.

That phoenix hell night,
I fell asleep in my clothes
on the red loveseat for one
with my mouth wide open
and my shoes still on,
and I dreamed of her in New York.

The next morning,
I awoke to a thousand missed phonecalls
indicated on my Canadian cellphone,
and somehow I knew,
something inside me knew
that this part of my life was at an awkward end.

I went to the store,
walking in yesterland's clothes,
and did my best at procrastinating the badnews.
I bought a scratch-off ticket and won five bucks
and I bought a big bottle of LaBatt's

and then I found out that my friend Michel
had died sometime during the night.

I thought it was my fault.
For a time.

I thought it was a drug overdose
or a coke-induced heart attack.

Nope.
He got hit by a truck on Rue LaMontagne.
He was trying to get to my house,
no doubt after banging some chick.
He would've crashed on the red loveseat
with his shoes on,
had he made it.

I went back to my place,
in the middle,
and did last night's dishes
and looked out the round window.

Back to the Past

Jack Johnson,
 and The Killers
bring me back
 to 2003...

Back to the swamp air,
sweetly, sweaty,
acrid
with ignorance.

If I die on Florida,
ship my inundated corpse
back to New York,
or Kansas, just don't bury me in Florida dirt.

Yacht Rock Christmas

It is a white Christmas, indeed.
Country Luke and I are blowing lines
while the ladies are making cookies
and pretending to be friends.

The leaves are gone, ignorant at best.
My boogers are already bloody.
I burn the turkey
while Country Luke slices up lines.

The gang listens to Steely Dan
and Rod Stewart and Sting,
and Liz Phair sneaks in there,
toss in Monty's mischief, we only see him on Christmas.

Fighting to be warm,
we order more online,
this is the twenty-first century,
even our father's could not have comprehended these
sidewalk-away trends.

We are money
with bones made of glass...
I know and so does Luke and Monty;
the ladies have no soup.

Let's retire to the foyer
and destroy the night.

Poem

Willful fork.
Willful hammer.
Willful window.
Willful exclamation point!

Listening to the Flame

woke at sunrise,
wished for more wishes and more eye-shut hours,
everyday,
with dreaming still on my demon mind.

woke at sunrise,
to a Burger King commercial haunting my living room,
and my living tongue tasted like last night's cocaine.

woke at sunrise,
took a train to Harlem
for a job interview (I didn't get the gig).

woke at sunrise,
with my mouth wide open,
still living in last night's shoes.

woke at sunrise,
on the kitchen floor, listening to the ConEd gas
of the pilot light.

woke at sunrise,
with nightmares still on my mind,
found a wheat penny in my back pocket.

woke at sunrise,
seeing the sun with hatred,
and a noose around my neck.

woke at sunrise,
with threatening weather, opening up for birds and
bishops, only,
and the meadowlarks are always listening to the flame
and the word.

One

the phone rings and I hear voices behind me and I spill
coffee on myself and then I decide to brush my teeth
and then I listen to folk music and skateboard in the
kitchen and then I go down on my girlfriend while she
is watching tv and I am eating her pussy because it
tastes so good and the evening is almost over and
Vernon is somewhere in the world smoking cigarettes
and his cellphone is off because he didn't pay the bill
and my lady is spreading her legs with the rest of them
on sad sacking earth and the moon is stolen by the
devil and the guitar kills itself and here I am fingering
and fucking and forgetting and finding out that more
wishes wished for is like breath seen in the morning as
it disappears over the lights and the cracks in the
concrete and the righteous men such as myself don't
give a fuck about anything being creatures with secrets
and muscles in their chests and who cares anyway.

Two

while all the fears I have cultivated throughout the
years kill themselves inside me on sad Monday
afternoons like today or yesterday, arrows and wind
make my window arms wave and drugs drag me down,
all the time riding in a car, a station wagon, with the
windows up and seatbelts are broken. kiss me in the
future as the world tilts on its axis and California falls
into the ocean not even making a jackknife splash or a
ripple in time, when we turn to burning down the sun
from our balconies, always giving up and giving in and
drugging, ketamine, and forgetting and wishing for
more wishes. this poetry is like eating dirt this poetry
is bullshit, nervous excitement and disgust make
mother's kitchen smell weird for a year, and tomorrow
Spanish speaking men will fight with me about my
mustache, and ultimately, like everyone else, like
California, I give up and give in and wish.

Jump Rivers

Got a job
in New Jersey
and the commute
is killing me.

I have high blood pressure.
A doctor has never
told me this
I just assume from
anger and sweaty palms
and fast food.

Doctors, like umbrellas,
and suicide attempts,
are for suckers.

Take pills to get high,
not to feel better.

I spill whiskey and cola
all over the crotch of my
work pants,
navy blue cords.

I was working
young
at a restaurant.

Second jobs
are mindless bastards,
as I bus tables and smoke weed
like sixteen, again,
and
the hardest part
is the PATH train,

but,
ultimately,
it doesn't
bother me at all,
and I already margined
one of the hosts,
a blonde named Tiffany,
she was either stupid
or easy,
not both.

Traveling back to Manhattan,
the way is tiresome and wrong
but the ghetto township
is round and welcoming
and sometimes I see shadows
of girls I have known
with tears and pseudo-fixed broken hearts.

The best part of this gig
is that it is
temporary,
like this year's September,
and
like last September's
newspaper gig
in Queens,
oh yeah.

NYC has the biggest ego in the world.
Two nights ago, I vomited on my shoes
while lost in the Bronx.
A hiding whiteboy,
I also threw-up while walking through the turnstile.

I work very hard.
Cocaine and adderall

make my heart work very hard.
Rain and cocaine made
me catch a cold.
Second jobs
help me afford drugs and dates.

I rest on a bench.

Past the factotum poet,
the shoreline ends.

Nothing Lasts

it's a funny thing
going back to Florida,
with it's strip malls
and humidity,
and realizing
the only thing
that changes is me.

my world
is extincting
and compounding
at the same time.

the city of mary
is pregnant again.

wasn't I sillier
back in the day?

now I know what
our parents were getting
on about,
saying that youth is lighter
than the ladder and the latter.

It is a damn shame
that nothing lasts
forever.

On the page it might.

Sometimes,
I also chase the sun,
my friend,
and these girls

are better off in my head.

Melt at her,
tremble.
 She wears my necklace around her wrist,
  doubled over, I vomit because I can't hold on to it all.

Sunday Vascular

addiction is like that...

cocaine Saturdays in general,
and/or preppy girls from Westchester County,
not to mention Panama City Beach,
or Chinese poetry.

next-days are blue
and spent vomiting,
not playing basketball,
always reading Chinese poetry.

I am him
who retreats to knuckles
and bottles
and words long dead from yesterday.

I am him
who gives up
and runs away
to LA.

this hornofplenty
needed here all the time,
slow Sunday
without sin.

I am him
who wonders why
Sunday feels like the last day of the week
and yet American man science says it is the first.

weird my arteries
with this fading love of wonderment
of today being today being today

185

and nothing but you and the best thing.

like we wrote before
in songs and poetry,
American, Mexican and Chinese,
autoharp my lips and forgive me.

Always the Lion Tamer

Under nicks
named stars
she hits me
up on the hip,

and roars softly, so softly,
that she wishes I were dead...

I could care less,

for I am
six nurses
and two criminals
into the opening scene
of the anti-climax
and she is clawless,
but for one claw.

However, the chair
is rusted
from rain and surreal,
evolutionary spite,
my heart is rusted, too.

The lion caught and ate a meadowlark.

The lion ate my whip.

I wished, that day,
that I had gotten
into the electric shark game
instead.

Satan! Satan! Satan!
my name is Leland,

I work with lions,
and I just saw you
in a shooting
star over the unquitting
river of grey eyes
and snake legs:
enjoy the regrets.

Shit Anecdote

When I was a junior in college
I scored a date with a gorgeous young girl,
we will call her Lana or Lindsay.

I picked her up in my two-toned 1986 Buick LeSabre
on a Saturday night,
she was wearing a denim skirt and Uggs,
she smelled good.

We went to a movie at the Waterford Lakes
multiplex and then we hit up
one of the casual dining chain restaurants
that dot the Central Florida landscape
like so many acne scars.

We were laughing the whole time.
There is not much in this world
better to me than making a girl laugh,
especially a good, real laugh.

When I was younger,
I learned early on
that I am not the best looking dude,
but I can be clever and funny
and that was my ticket
into the world and pants of the opposite sex.

Back to the date,
I excused myself from the table
and proceeded to the restroom.
I was finishing a piss
when sneaky flatulence came up and out
but was not alone!
I had just accidentally shit my pants.

In a panic, I zipped up and forgot to wash my hands.
I went back to the table
and when I sat down
I became painfully aware of the severity of the
situation.
I felt the warm pudding smash in my boxer shorts and
jeans.
I was sweating and no longer able to be funny.
Being young and dumb, I hastily paid the tab
and ushered us the fuck out of there,
giving Lana or Lindsay a lame excuse about having
class in the morning.
I drove her home in silence.
She must've been so goddamned confused
in her mind as to how a joker like me
was offing a girl like her without any excuse at all.

What could I have said?
"Sorry, Lana or Lindsay, but I just shit my pants and
now I must go home and change."
No fucking way.
I never saw her again.
I later heard she moved back to Miami.

Billy the Ghost

Billy was a ghost,
in a summary of power
and jurisdiction,
dancing in her attic.

Rudy never set eyes on him,
only heard his footsteps and voice.
She lived alone
or so she thought.

Maybe he is homesick,
Rudy thought after months
of research and records
of Kew Gardens, Queens, NY residents.

Billy the human
had grown up in this house.
He died of consumption
in the winter of 1893 in Manhattan.

Billy the human is in
the west wing of the Maple Grove Cemetery.
Billy the ghost is in
his old room in Rudy's attic.

Painted Poetic Hours

my left hand smells of gasoline.
my two front teeth are loose.
my right eye twitches.

bought eggs and coffee with nickels.
bought drugs with a credit card.
happy, mellow, face music.

take a picture of the morning with my cellphone.
send a letter to the woman I love.
it says 'Baby, I am sorry.'

call my sister, she doesn't pick up.
CD player, *The Weakerthans*.
coloring in coloring books.

drunk at work.
see death always then.
ascending like lime tree truths.

Conway Acres

Abercorn,
take the first two
harp rights,
past the big yard
with the tree house;

past the white supremacists,
past the Latin Eagles
and the Latin Kings:
both members of Folk Nation;

past the swamp
and the tadpoles who know,
and the fence,
behind which the kidnappers hide,
and the pitbull on a chain
in a yard without a fence
(it is only a matter of time);

you'll enter a trailer park
in the back,
past the retention pond,
past the second basketball hoop,
the one with the chain net;

past rednecks with their white trash wives
with their country music playing,
and the trailers with lawns so long
the entire lot looks like Jurassic Park
which Carlos and I just saw for the fifth time
for free
at the Hoffner Center 6;

we snuck in
the same day Darrell

193

ripped his nostril while trying to dunk
on the first basketball hoop,
the one with the chain link net.

Take your last left
onto Chickadee Avenue
and we are the third trailer
on the left, just past said basketball hoop
with the chain net:
1462 Chickadee Avenue.
I mowed that lawn,
front and back.
There are hamsters and fish and
we built that fence in the backyard,
this is where we all died,
myself, for the first time.

My best friend, Carlos, lived next-door
with his sisters: Laura and Joanna and Jessica
and their mother, Miriam.
They gave us a kitten
and baseball cards, once or twice,
and sugar,
and I mowed their lawn, too.

Symphony Asleep Through This Holy Cannon Duke

sing.
sick queen.
ten things.
weak end Wednesdays.
One hundred and sixty two dreams
without numbers.

"I skipped a Turkish dinner for this."

You be me for a bit
and I will be your dumb skull,
romantic at best.

Over.
Asleep
Holy.
And.
Yours.

"I write poems like Paul Westerberg wrote songs."

have you ever apologized twice?

Certainly.
In red.
Or maroon.
Or death.

I write poems like Sidney Offit rides the crosstown bus."

Everyday.
Loud.
Lit.
Metaphorical.
Pistol and knife.

Windows.
Hammers.
Legs.
Symphony.

There is a hole in the drapes
east of the living room
and
I am already where I am from:
the cannon.

Time Capsule

I.
To the future,
are you humans?
or spiders?
yellow or African?

is the internet still around?

we are writing from the December of 2011 a.d.

I apologize for my transgressions.

II.
To the future,
I don't believe in you.
you'll never amount to anything.
I resent you.

you are the reason the world shakes,
not me.

rape is always an option.

Self-Titled Conspirator

this is nothing new.

Inkwind.
Xylophone.
Tonight,
I am a rhapsode.

So I guess I got old.

'Hope regenerates'.

Why do I ask why
so many times in the night?

I ain't done a damn thing right.
Believe me, I wish I were dead.
But I will never be able to live with myself
if I ever stop trying.

Fate won't fix this.

Tomorrow, I will die in a doorway
while trying to reach
the driveway with a letter in hand.

Chipped a tooth on your heart.

tell ourselves that this is love,
when it is actually everything.

it is the only luck we know how to live.

make a mess of good grace.
try to drink the clock backwards.

whiskey werds.
never. stop.
it. learned.
some day.

it is the only luck we know how to live.

Canyon
(for New York City)

Winner.
Wants/Needs.
Full.
Unintelligent.

I am a coffee.
and a ska band.
and Harlem.
Settling into myselves.

I take everything
because I am in love.
with a town known
to the sun as doom.

If I destroy myself
somewhere else,
please God,
bring my inundated corpse back here.

Whispering:
The beginning of time.
Maybe these are mountains
I see towering over me.

I am a womb.
and a son.
And a wolf.
Of the center.
Of the universe.
I know what to call this town:

Bishopric.
Avarice.

A canyon.
Tipsy.
Me.

the angles
in this
godforsaken place
make it great.

it is a desert
but it is not
the same colors
as a desert.

it is three thousand
five hundred and two miles
from lies and weekends,
Manhattan, goddamn it.

Poems are too
goddamn heavy
to carry around
this canyon!

This Is Not The End!

I.

this is not the end.
this is not the end.
this is not the end.
this is not the end.

this is not the end.
this is not the end.
this is not the end.
this is not the end!

maybe it is.
maybe it is the Day of the Dead.
or the anniversary of my birth.
or a ripple or a stitch.

this is not the end.
I'll see her in the middle.
if I make it there.
one hundred and sixty two points.

this is not the end.
you ever wake up.
on a day in which everything.
everything is going so wrong?

this is not the end?
nope.
everything is so wrong.
that you get terribly happy.

this is not the end!
because what else could get worse.
the love we made.

at gunpoint, indeed.

this is not the end!
for I am just a gardener.
like she said yesterday in Brooklyn.
maybe a runner or a spy, indeed.

II.

there are bones in my soul
and two of the ribs just broke
from a heart and a stomach
both of which can't decide
what the other wants to be:
a goblin or a nigger,
or a ripple or a stitch in time or a pebble.

my mom took me to the hospital
and the doctor seemed so sad
like years of bad luck had broken his mirrors
and now he has to cut into a kid
and tell him that his heart is a goblin
and his stomach is actually his liver
and his liver is actually an old helicopter.

silence sings in the desert
and disappears in my eyes
both of which are turning inside out
like a sheep in October,
like a slumbering villain
with words in the ground.

this surface is useless,
like colors in water,
and regrets from last year;
this chopper is my abdomen
and the inside is red and brown

and I never see the changes.

Seasons until something is turned outside in like eyes,
outside of which sinner leaves fall on sinner ground
in the fall/winter fever of two-day drinks and riddles
like this one and the bones of my soul,
hollow as they were under poison fog
while questioning every wind.

Red-breasted robins are not alive,
neither is the alehouse child,
just ghosts along the trail
for sale for passersby,
caroling about targets
and waiting to die.

neither am I.

the fingers typing this today (yesterday)
are forgotten timbers low in command
careful not to have the Sheppard
who is blind and frightened
and locked inside my bullshit barrel chest
share everything;
covered by lightning so sharp
splitting windows and ribs,
it ceases to be seen at all
under blood and sunburned suburbs
which sit under god and east of hillsides.

III.

it is cold
in here
with wine
and allowing-memory.

bastard in the wake of the eyes.
what about two cool things?
in a row!?
her and her and her and sponsorship from the five
boroughs.
kill me now?
nope.
this is not the end.
Lives are lived in a row.
no internet as the streets, hear coyotes call,
like throwing old lazy poems at the murdered moon,
just like me, drunk and reckless,
assholed in the morning time, tome.

IV.

inside the liver
with yellow teeth
Monday's noon is today's
metaphor for wasted youth,
slowly dripping off bones
just as time allows death to be scene from balconies.

no such shallower graves as this
than such a neighborhood on fire,
raised by bottom moms and cupid.
so when I die I will be buried
in loose sand near the bay.

give a thought or two
to the Her that I know,
wonder why the path taken
has lead us here, for good or ill.

sad as the lingering ghosts
of memory amongst memories,
apoidea apoidea apoidea,

this is not the end.

I say this over and over and smoke cigarettes.

V.

as the day lines (or lining) up...
there and then not.
In a taxi cab for a moment.
In a bar for an afternoon.

putting all my power
into kissing her goodbye,
because this may or may not
be the very last time.

contradictory to the snow
my heart is melting...
almost in love
almost throwing up.
the love we made,
the dancing in the moon,
my mind is a hoarder's room
in a magnetic parking lot.
My memories are metal.
I watch you watch me
in another time.
I scream from the very top
of an eastern mountain.
I scream from a city near the sea,
about things I have seen.

contradictory to the phone's purpose
my ringing vernacular is Sunday's truth...
the lines of thoughts like
one day being there and one day not,
like Mexican pilgrims

like love in a telescope;
my lawn grows freckles
in a magnetic parking lot.
I wait for you waiting for me,
invisible all along,
I search from south to east
of everywhere today, a bullshit bullet
in my *TNT* barrel heart under my heart under my soul,
covered in bone fragments from sad freedom.

contradictory to my mind
as a dentist's waiting room —
wait! I have done this very thing before —
inconsistent either within itself or the snow,
my heart is an empty stomach,
as I just sit here and wait and wait and wait
and wait and wait and wait and wait
for something to happen,
holding opposite dogs, baby,
braid my hair another time,
fond of given views for now,
breasts and birthdays and burials,
all the things, like immemorial memories in between
me and you.

from now on,
everything that happens,
will not be as sweet
as yesterday morning.

VI.

this is dogwood.
this is doing the dishes.
this is addiction.
this is love.
this is repetition.

this is my life.
this is baffling.
this is Taiwanese poetry.
this is cornflower blue.
this is the stars.
this is a blanket.
this is heaven.
this is black lightning.
this is the trail.
this is salt.
this is a love song.
this is sweeping.
this is what you are seeing.
this is high.
this is loud.
this is pride.
this is every little word.
this is absurd.
this is prayer.
this is *Bon Iver*.
this is prison.
this is remembering.
this is gospel.
this is raucous.
this is time, for sure.

this is not the end.

VII.

this is the wind.
this is my father.
this is not Los Angeles.
this is willpower.
this is loneliness.
this is cocaine.
this is love.

this is not New York.
this is a hammer.
this is kismet.
this is a tomahawk.
this is birthdays.
this is suicide.
this is music.
this is ears.
this is eyes.
this is the world.
this is your feet.
this is the end.
this is the age of seventeen.
this is two-headed.
this is choking.
this is the beginning.

this is not the end.

VIII.

this is stained glass.
this is offended.
this is a fork.
this is guy and girl.
this is not Montreal.
this is the color yellow.
this is an exclamation point.
this is letting go.
this is whiskey.
this is television.
this is regret.
this is joy.
this is permission.
this is pessimism, at its best.
this is a window.
this is not Florida.

this is anti-heroism.
this is rain.
this is childhood home.
this is blood from the coyote.
this is blame.
this is having wings.
this is stone gossip.
this is happiness.
this is shadows.
this is memories.
this is the truth.

this is not the end.
this is this.

VVI.

underneath it all,
skeletons and all,
we are there (here) and then we are not,
like lions underground,
sweating out screams,
roaring through sad fake trees for dinner tonight,
only tonight, indeed.

My binge heights Mondays
spent falling in love with girls
in New York City, and everywhere else,
yes indeed,
that too will be the past
as time never stops,
heart then head,
live,
enjoy the regrets.

dasein.
sufferer.

song.
myself.

as the building(s) rise
I know nothing about time
or what makes wind,
I do know
that this is not the end.
the world does not hate you,
but it doesn't like you either.
I do, though, and so does she.
The Brazilian.
the sky
in the sky.
the things we have seen
there (here).

X.

the bastion behind eyes
and a future heart attack
killed any chance of changing the world,
and yet I know I will be alright,
but what about her or him
and come to think of it,
will I be alright?

Dead soon?
Heart attack?
Who says?

snake in song wild
caught in a snake trip
by Jib the Killer
or Jib the Lawyer.
beat the Mayan Sun, my son, too,
calendar with anti freeze

caught under cars
with combustible engines
in magnetic parking lots
in Florida and Brazil and other places
most of which god forgets about.

sometimes while I am driving
in the near past, daydreams designed by the Devil,
three years ago, maybe,
I saw rose covered bodies
lying in the street
with their backs to my head lights.
I was asleep at the wheel.
I never thought I would be here (there).

XI.

deaf and dumb dear bones
under soul,
ribs with rain
as children
coming home
from way way out there.

they care
like anybody else,
cold and naïve,
but altogether human
like angels with genitalia,
and the Buddhist fever in their sheepish eyes
which cracks in red—
that they will eventually
die.

what is this, then?
this is a feather.
this is a bondi ornament.

this is a different font.
I've said what this is.
this is none of your fucking business.
this is not the end.
subsequently.
This is today.
This is now.
This is morning.
I woke up again
on the twenty-sixth day
of October
in the foul year of our lord,
nineteen and eighty-two.
I dreamed of Existentialism.